To Mr & Mrs. Maggs,

with very best wishes

The Royal Hundred of Bray

Written by Luke Over

Illustrated by Chris Tyrrell

Published & Printed by Cliveden Press
Priors Way, Bray, Maidenhead, Berkshire SL6 2HP
Tel: Maidenhead (0628) 75151 Fax: (0628) 773090

1993

Copyright © Text Luke Over, 1993
Copyright © Illustrations Chris Tyrrell, 1993

ISBN 0 9521969 0 5

Preface

This is the first book to be written on Bray Hundred since *The History and Antiquities of the Hundred of Bray* by Charles Kerry in 1861. Mr. Kerry was the headmaster of the Bray and Holyport School, and all local historians are indebted to him for the painstaking research he carried out at the time. It is a book written by an academic for academics and no doubt had a small circulation, being written at a time when general education was in its infancy.

In 1973 the late Nan Birney, a local resident, wrote *Bray, Today and Yesterday*, a popular account of the village and Braywick, mainly over the past 150 years. In her preface Mrs. Birney admits that she was not an historian, and hoped that one day somebody would write a fuller account of the history of Bray.

During the past twenty years there has been an increased interest in local history from those people who like to relate to their environment. The demand seems to be for academic facts presented in a popular way, and this is what the authors have tried to achieve in *The Royal Hundred of Bray*.

The book tells the story of Bray Hundred since its evolution in the Ice Ages, and chronologically through to the present day. After settlement in the Prehistoric and Roman periods, Bray emerged as a royal manor when the Saxon King Edmund I was residing at his palace at Old Windsor. Throughout the medieval period Bray was part of the Queen's dower and mainly under control of the Crown and the Abbey of Cirencester.

In compiling this book the authors have combined evidence from primary and secondary sources, ancient documents, excavation, fieldwork and placenames. Much of the evidence is new and some may find the hypotheses presented surprising or even controversial. Either way the book will be a definitive history of Bray until it is superseded at some time in the future.

The authors are also aware of the need for illustration, and to this end have provided over 70 high quality line drawings of buildings and scenes in the locality. Some of the buildings are well known, others lesser known, whilst some have now been demolished. Reconstructions from the early periods are based on archaeological knowledge and the results of excavations. Maps have been included to pinpoint local features.

In the production of this book the authors would like to thank Peter Morris for his faith in its success, Veronica Kempton for the typescript, and the Rev. George Repath, Vicar of Bray, for writing the Foreword, which is particularly relevant this year which marks the 700th Anniversary of Bray Church.

Foreword

Not since 1861, the year when Charles Kerry's *The History and Antiquities of the Hundred of Bray* was published, has anyone attempted to write a full history of the Parish of Bray. Luke Over is to be highly complimented on his tremendous achievement in updating Kerry's work, and filling in gaps which were unremarked upon for various reasons, more than a century ago. This book, with its excellent illustrations by Chris Tyrrell of so many of the buildings and features described in it, is a tribute to the local historians' painstaking research, and great love for their subject. All who read these pages will find their knowledge of Bray, and its history, much enriched.

The Reverend George Repath,
Vicar of Bray

Bray Church in Winter

About the Authors

The writer, Luke Over, is acknowledged as a local historian and is well known for his lectures and the 200 articles he has written for the *Maidenhead Advertiser*. After studying archaeology at London University he spent 30 years excavating sites in the area and elsewhere including the Domesday site of Maidenhead. In the past 15 years he has concentrated on the history of the area, carrying out fieldwork, studying placenames and examining old documents, in the hope of discovering new facts about the early history of east Berkshire.

His literary achievements in this field include numerous articles for journals, local and national magazines and some 44 publications. His books *The Story of Maidenhead*, *Maidenhead – A Pictorial History* and *Domesday Revisited* proved to be popular best sellers on the local market, whilst *Furze Platt Remembered*, which he ghost wrote for Ray Knibbs, sold out in ten days.

In the past year he has been talking about local history in a series of programmes on B.B.C. Radio Berkshire. He is Secretary of the Berkshire Archaeological Society and a Vice President of the Maidenhead Archaeological & Historical Society, as well as serving on numerous other committees. His ambition is to promote an interest in local history and an understanding of the local environment.

The illustrator, Chris Tyrrell, was born at Hayes in Middlesex and studied art at the Twickenham College of Technology. After his initial training and during the 1960s he was guided in his work by the royal portrait painter Pietro Annigoni. During his career he has travelled extensively in Europe and the Far East producing paintings and sketches in Thailand, Hong Kong and China.

His paintings have been exhibited at the Royal Society of Portrait Painters, the Royal Society of British Artists, the Royal Society of Painter-Etchers and Engravers, the United Society of Artists and the Royal Institute Summer Salon. He is an elected member of the Society of Architectural Illustrators.

His one-man exhibition 'Around Maidenhead' in 1988 was opened by Her Grace the Duchess of Norfolk, on which occasion he presented a painting of Pine Lodge to the Thames Valley Hospice.

Much of his local work has been published as Christmas cards, calendars, postcards and in magazines. His paintings of Cookham were used in the book *The Story of Cookham*. Many of his paintings are in collections worldwide and various notable personalities collect his work. At present he is concentrating on landscapes and architectural subjects in watercolours.

Contents

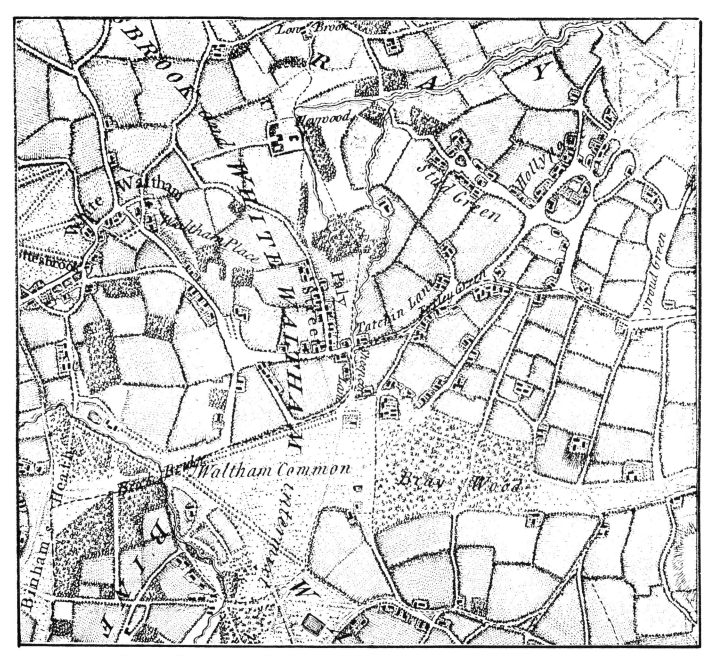

Holyport and South Bray (John Rocque c 1761)

CHAPTER I

Introducing the Royal Hundred

To the casual visitor who might be tempted to step ashore from a moored boat on the Thames, the village of Bray must appear to be very small and compact. A walk along Ferry Lane will lead them to the short High Street flanked by numerous protected buildings, some dating back to 1400. Another hundred yards will lead them to the fifteenth century Lych Gate, where many funeral parties have gathered over the centuries. On passing through the thirteenth century church will come into view, conjuring up an image of the infamous Vicar of Bray, known from the proverb to be a Tudor turncoat. Most would be satisfied with this perambulation and consider that they had walked the full extent of the settlement and taken in its history.

However, as most will know, the parish of Bray extends over a large area and is bordered by the parishes of Clewer to the east, Winkfield and Warfield to the south and Waltham to the west. A large proportion of the northern section was absorbed into the town of Maidenhead but at one time the boundary stretched from the Shire Horse on Maidenhead Thicket to the Bridge on the line of the old Bath Road and through the centre of Maidenhead High Street.

The division of land into territorial units as we see them today began in the Anglo-Saxon era. These took the form of administrative areas under either ecclesiastical or civil control. The unit of ecclesiastical control was the parish, the earliest of which were created in the sixth century with the coming of St. Augustine to Britain. The first parishes normally covered a wide area, dependent on the number of churches available for worship. The earliest type of parish church was the minster, which was usually a royal or episcopal foundation, under the control of a number of priests. As more churches became available from endowments provided by the upper classes, additional parishes were created making administration more manageable. In the early stages these were under the control of a rector rather than a vicar.

Before the eighth century A.D. Britain was divided into *provinciae*, the earliest known units of local government which originated from Roman times. By the year 800, Wessex at least had been divided up into *shires*, or counties, much as we see them today. These in turn were sub-divided into *hundreds*, which were notionally an area of 100 hides of land, or 12,000 acres, but in practice were not usually that precise. Within the hundreds were a series of *manors*, smaller self-sufficient agricultural units, which in most cases have developed into modern villages. Each manor was controlled by a tenant-in-chief who held a manor house, and consisted of arable, meadow and woodland and were situated near water, mills and fisheries. Where manors coincided with parishes there was also a parish church.

Bray can now be considered within the context of these early boundaries. The parish of Bray may well have been formed in the seventh century as Christianity was introduced in Wessex and the Thames Valley in AD634 by Birinus, a bishop from Rome, who formed a *see* at Dorchester-on-Thames. In the following year he baptised the Wessex leader Cynegils and began his conversion throughout the Thames Valley. Tradition has it that local baptism took place at the Bapsey Pond near Taplow Court. The existence of a pre-conquest church at Bray cannot be confirmed with certainty, the first mention of a building being in the Domesday Survey of c1086. However, evidence suggests that Bray may have been a minster because of its royal foundation.

Before it became a shire the east of Berkshire including Bray was part of the provincia of *Suninges*, and came under the Bishopric of Salisbury. The vast ecclesiastical estate spread from the present village of Sonning for some distance to the west and eastwards as far as Sunninghill, which derives its name from the same source. There was a church at Sonning in the ninth century when Saxon bishops resided there. The site of the Bishop's Palace was excavated earlier this century and showed an occupation from the tenth century until the dissolution around 1547.

The first mention of Berkshire as a county was in AD860 when it was recorded as *Berrocscir* and took its name from a wood near Hungerford. The earliest details of the county are given in the Domesday Survey c1086 where it is shown that the shire was sub-divided into 22 hundreds which in turn were broken up into 192 manors. Although this indicates an average of 9 manors per hundred, the largest had 15 and Bray Hundred was unique in that the hundred and manor had the same acreage and name, in contrast with the two neighbouring hundreds of Beynhurst and Ripplesmere which had 7 manors in each. Bray was the smallest of the Berkshire hundreds and was taxed in 1086 as 2,281 acres whilst the acreage recorded in 1905 was a total of 7,820 which included 2,208 of arable land, 4,690 of permanent grass and 492 of woodland.

The reason for this discrepancy probably lies in the fact that right through the medieval period Bray remained a Royal manor and Hundred, and therefore only part of the area was subject to taxation. Bray's royal tag seems to go back as far as AD942, when the principal manor was vested in the Crown. In that year the Saxon King Edmund I 'granted the meadow of *Hockesham* by charter to the Abbot of Abingdon, and for this meadow each succeeding abbot did homage to the King at the manorial court at Bray'. At the same time King Edmund made grants in the neighbouring manors of Winkfield and Waltham.

Royal interest in the hundred and manor of Bray is due to its proximity to the palace and castle at Windsor. The Domesday Book mentions the palace of the Saxon kings at Old Windsor and the 95 *hagae* or house plots that surrounded the palace complex and were in use as residences for the officials of the court. This palace is often attributed to Edward the Confessor (1042–66) but could conceivably have been in use in the time of Edmund I (940–46). The castle at New Windsor was built in 1070 in the manor of Clewer for the defence of the realm, but succeeded the palace at Old Windsor as a royal residence when Henry I took over the building in the year 1110.

The hundred of Bray would have been a convenient spot to house any royal officials, tenants-in-chief or Knights who needed to commute on a regular basis to Windsor Castle, remembering that they would be travelling by horse. Bray was also adjacent to the Forest of Windsor, an area set aside for the King's hunting activities. At the time of the Domesday Survey the forest was mainly confined to the Windsor area, but William

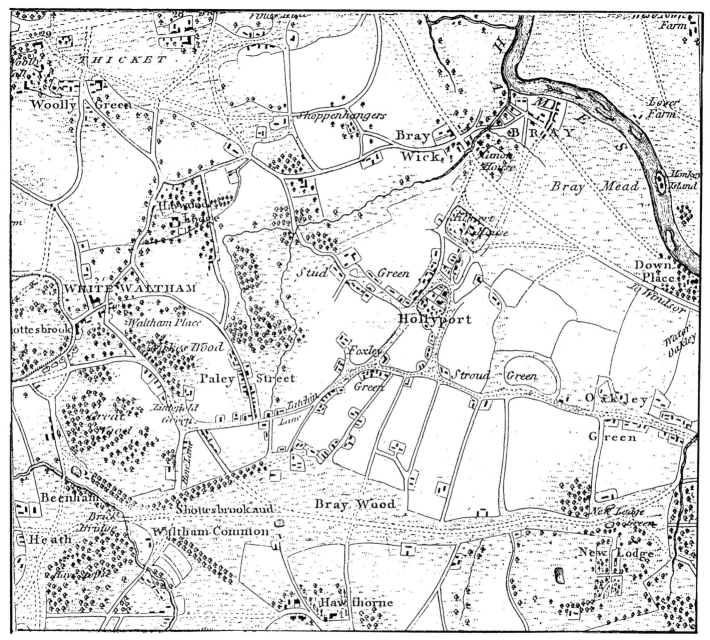

The Royal Hundred of Bray (Thomas Pride c. 1791)

I and subsequent Norman kings extended the bounds until a large area of East Berkshire was taken up. In the chronicles of Abingdon Abbey there is a reference to how William turned the abodes of men into habitation for beasts at Winkfield. On the Norden map of 1607 the circuit of the Forest is shown to be 77 miles.

In 1225 a perambulation of east Berkshire by the Forest justices led to the formation of the Liberty of the Forest, later known as the Liberty of the Seven Hundreds and then by 1296 as the Seven Hundreds of Cookham and Bray. The court associated with this was the chief court for the forest district, and the seven hundreds were those of Cookham, Bray, Ripplesmere, Beynhurst, Wargrave, Sonning and Charlton. Apparently the idea of this was to ensure uniform administration of the forest area and its royal game and to inflict severe penalties on anyone interfering with them. In 1268 Roger de Fryht was appointed bailiff of the

The Seven Hundreds of Cookham and Bray (Robert Morden c. 1695)

Seven Hundreds and he was succeeded by Ralph de Waltham in 1311.

Despite the fact that Bray is the only settlement mentioned in the Hundred of Bray in Saxon and Norman times, the area embraces many other communities which are known to have existed in early times. Their history will be described later but they include Oakley Green, East Oakley, Water Oakley, Fifield, Holyport, Stud Green, Touchen End, Moneyrow Green, Braywick and Hawthorn Hill. Other settlements now merged with Maidenhead include Cox Green, Altwood, Tittle Row, Boyn Hill, Oldfield and the Fisheries.

Before completing this introduction to the Hundred the name of Bray should be discussed. Early variants include *Brai, Bras 1086, Braya 1160, Brai Regis 1167*, indicating the royal connection, and *Braye 1220*. To most etymologists the meaning of the name has been the subject of controversy, and

Bray Enclosure Map c. 1817

none can agree whether the origins lie in Old English or French. There are numerous Brays in England, Ireland and France all of which are topographically different. The Hundred of Bray is basically a very flat area with little land rise and the areas close to the river were, at one time, always subject to annual flooding.

Kerry maintains that the name derives from the Norman french work *Braium*, meaning a Marsh or Moist Place, and cites other Bray settlements situated on the French rivers Seine, Somme and Epte. In each of these places the terrain is flat and marshy and in all ways similar to Bray in Berkshire.

The English Place Names Society still remains undecided about the meaning. Like Kerry they quote a twelfth century old French word *Braye* commonly meaning 'mud', which in all respects is similar. However, other Bray settlements in the United Kingdom are said to derive from the Old English *breg* meaning the 'brow (of a hill)'. Topographically speaking, this derivation on the face of it would appear unacceptable, unless some special significance can be attributed to Canon Hill, Hawthorn Hill or Boyn Hill which are at some distance from the main settlement. At present the actual meaning of the name Bray must remain obscure.

THE VICAR OF BRAY.

The author of this celebrated composition is said to have been an officer in Colonel Fuller's regiment in the time of George I.

"In good King Charles's golden days,
　When loyalty had no harm in't,
A zealous High Churchman I was,
　And so I got preferment.
To teach my flock I never miss'd
　Kings were by God appointed,
And they are damned who dare resist,
　Or touch the Lord's anointed.
　　Chorus— And this is law I will maintain,
　　　　　Until my dying day, sir,
　　　　　That whatsoever king shall reign,
　　　　　I'll be the Vicar of Bray, sir.

"When Royal James obtained the throne,
　And Popery grew in fashion,
The penal laws I hooted down,
　And read the Declaration;
The Church of Rome I found would fit
　Full well my constitution;
And I had been a Jesuit,
　But for the Revolution.

"When William, our deliverer, came
　To heal the nation's grievance,
Then I turned cat-in-pan again,
　And swore to him allegiance.
Old principles I did revoke,
　Set conscience at a distance;
Passive obedience was a joke,
　A jest was non-resistance.

"When glorious Anne became our Queen,
　The Church of England's glory,
Another face of things was seen,
　And I became a Tory.

Occasional conformist's case—
　I damned such moderation;
And thought the Church in danger was
　By such prevarication.

"When George in pudding-time came o'er,
　And moderate men looked big, sir,
My principles I changed once more,
　And so—became a Whig, sir.
And thus preferment I procured
　From our Faith's Great Defender,
And almost every day adjured
　The Pope and the Pretender.

"The illustrious House of Hanover,
　And Protestant Succession,
By these I lustily will swear,
　While they can keep possession:
For in my faith and loyalty
　I never once will falter,
But George my king shall ever be—
　Except the times do alter."

CHAPTER II

Bray Genesis

The landscape of Bray as we see it today was fashioned during a series of Ice Ages which occurred in the last 500,000 years of geological time. The solid geology of chalk and flint was laid down as crushed seashells and marine organisms below the Cretaceous Seas some 200 million years ago. These time spans are perhaps difficult for us to envisage, and the reality that the Thames once flowed on a level with Winter Hill and Cookham Dean is even more difficult to imagine.

In the last half million years there have been three glaciations and three interglacial periods, during which time the Thames flowed alternatively fast or slow depending on the amount of water. The Thames Valley itself was carved from the chalk to a depth of 150 feet by fast flowing torrents when the ice was melting, whilst forming a series of flood plains during the times when the river was more stable. These flood plains occur as gravel terraces at varying heights above the present river level and are named after places in the Bray area because of the early studies carried out there.

The highest Thames terraces are the oldest and occur as Winter Hill (150 feet), Boyn Hill (100 feet), Lynch Hill or Furze Platt (65 feet), Taplow (40 feet) and the present flood plain. It was on these terraces that the nomadic hunter-gatherers of the Old Stone Age, or *Palaeolithic* period first erected their flimsy shelters of wood and animal hide, and fashioned stone tools and hand axes from the abundant supply of flint in the area.

As can be seen from the published map, the main terraces occurring in the Hundred of Bray are those of Taplow and Boyn Hill, with various deposits associated with the

Mesolithic Camp

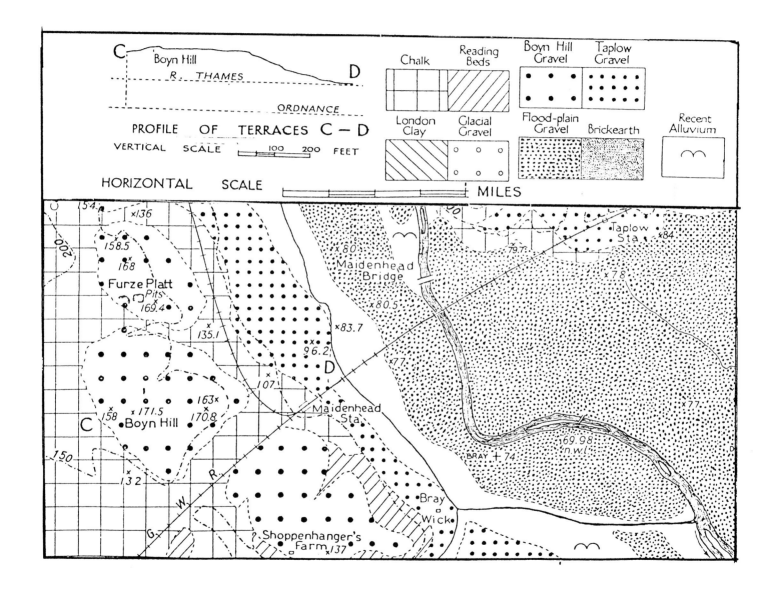

C Boyn Hill D

R. THAMES

ORDNANCE

PROFILE OF TERRACES C–D

VERTICAL SCALE 100 200 FEET

HORIZONTAL SCALE MILES

Chalk | Reading Beds | Boyn Hill Gravel | Taplow Gravel

London Clay | Glacial Gravel | Flood-plain Gravel | Brickearth

Recent Alluvium

154.a
×136
158.5
×168
Furze Platt
Pits
169.4
135.1
×83.7
×96.2
×107
D
×163
×171.5
170.8
158 ·Boyn Hill
C
150
×132
G.W.R.
Shoppenhanger's Farm ×137

Maidenhead Bridge
×80.
×80.5
×77
Maidenhead Sta.
Bray Wick
BRAY +74
169.98 n.w.l.
×77

79.7
Taplow Sta. ×84
×78

present flood plain. Over the past one hundred years gravel extraction on these terraces has produced large quantities of stone axes and tools of this remote period which can date to anything from 350,000 to 10,000 BC, depending on their stratification. The whole *Palaeolithic* period is subject to numerous sub-divisions which are not relevant to discuss here. At Cannon Court Pit, Furze Platt, over 2,000 stone axes have been recovered, and an indeterminate number on the summit of Boyn Hill during the Victorian era. Even with the advanced state of modern archaeology, we can only guess at the lifestyle of these early nomads, as stone implements are all that survive.

Mesolithic, or Middle Stone Age man appears to have migrated from the Continent around 10,000 BC and radiocarbon dates from their occupation in Berkshire range from 8415 BC at Thatcham Down to 3310 BC at Wawcott, in the Kennet Valley. In contrast to *Palaeolithic* Man, these new settlers appeared to be dependent on fish as the main ingredient of their diet. This does not mean that they did not hunt animals, but with a warmer climate it is likely that in some places forest extended down to the river's edge, making access difficult. Whilst the Thames pick took the place of the earlier handaxe, the main assemblage of tools took the form of *microliths*, or minute stone tools, which when hafted were suitable for the spearing of fish.

These settlers appeared after the final glaciation and therefore their settlements are to be found on the present flood plains. Strangely enough the Thames flood plain has yielded little or no *Mesolithic* occupation, and on present evidence it would appear that settlement sites are confined to smaller rivers, streams and tributaries. In Bray a major site of this period was excavated in 1970 adjacent to The Cut at Braywick (SU.894791). This small tributary should be more correctly known as Shaffelmoor Stream and flows across an area which was at one time boggy land.

Despite the layers of peaty soil the excavation did not reveal surviving organic materials or evidence of early wooden dwellings of this period. However, in common with other sites in the county, several flint working surfaces were uncovered and some 10,000 flints recovered, many of which were actual microliths. Their type and manufacture suggested that these were flint tools of the *Maglemosian* culture, a sub-division of the *Mesolithic* period, which cannot be accurately dated at Bray.

By 4000 BC, after Britain had become separated from the Continent, the people of the New Stone Age, or *Neolithic* period, had arrived in the Thames Valley. These were the first farmers in Britain and were looking for arable land on which to cultivate their crops of wheat, emmer and spelt, early cereals which had been developed in the Middle East. The implements of this period, whilst still made of flint and stone, were much more sophisticated. Axes were smooth and polished and in some cases hafted, whilst flint arrowheads were designed for hunting. Picks fashioned from deer antlers were used as a digging tool, and other items were manufactured from bone. Many artifacts of this period have been dredged from the Thames and located during gravel extraction on the flood plain at Bray.

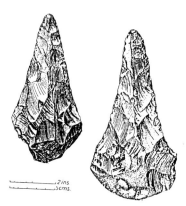

The *Neolithic* peoples brought with them the first signs of any social organisation. Wooded areas were cleared to provide arable land, animals were domesticated, and circular wooden huts were built to provide dwellings from which to control their smallholdings. One of their major innovations was the introduction of pottery, in which they could store food and water, containers for which had previously been made from animal hides.

Palaeolithic Handaxes

The main site of this period in Bray was found when Canon Hill House was demolished and the Binghams housing estate built (SU.897794). Whilst excavating the rubbish pits of the old house for examples of eighteenth century pottery, two deep shafts were noted in the cellars. On closer examination it was revealed that the shafts were dug for an unknown purpose during the *Neolithic* period. Close to the top of one shaft which had gone out of use and silted up, was a hearth, built by Stone Age man, and containing carbon, bone and many sherds of crude pottery. The pottery, when assembled, proved to be the remains of some five pots with sagging bases, and was dated from a radiocarbon sample of the charcoal to 3340 BC. This is still today probably the earliest pottery ever found in Britain. If one compares this date with the later date of 3310 BC for *Mesolithic* activity in the Kennet Valley, it can be seen that *Neolithic* and *Mesolithic* people may have lived side by side for a period of time.

At this stage it should perhaps be said that during the prehistoric era the settlers in Bray Hundred were mainly concerned with farming and there are no examples of the major monuments that occur in other parts of southern England. These include the large earthworks like the causewayed camps and henge monuments of the *Neolithic* and the hillforts of the *Iron Age*. Neither are there any chambered *Neolithic* burial mounds or round barrows of the *Bronze Age* used for the interment of notable families. In Bray, it would seem, the inhabitants were everyday people, ekeing out a living, who were cremated or buried in flat graves when their day came.

The sub-division of the prehistoric period has for a long time tended to be named after materials used for the manufacture of their implements. The long usage of stone for making effective but rather cumbersome tools came to an end in 1800 BC when bronze smiths from the Mediterranean brought to Britain the knowledge of metal working. The tools of the *Bronze Age* were sophisticated for their time and the old handaxe was replaced by socketed metal axeheads which when hafted were much easier to use. Along with these were an assemblage of knives, swords, rapiers and other weapons which could be efficiently used in times of combat. Numerous examples of these have been found close to Monkey Island Lane and Bray Marina.

One important site of this period was excavated in 1991 at Weir Bank Farm, near Monkey Island (SU.911791) prior to gravel extraction. Evidence from the dig revealed a number of ditched enclosures, probably paddocks or small fields, situated on the Thames flood plain. Originally the ditches may have been for the irrigation of crops and probably had the effect of forming small islands making territorial sub-division. On one island a timber-built roundhouse with porch was defined by a ring of post-holes, whilst nearby was found further holes representing the supports for a small granary. Apart from numerous finds dating to around 100 BC, the site yielded large quantities of animal bone and a number of cremations in individually buried pits on the edge of the complex. Many pits dug into the ground were used for storage of grain and waste disposal.

Evidence of the following *Iron Age* period, when the new metal came into use, is sparse in Bray. No farmsteads of this period have yet been located and evidence is mainly confined to broken pottery spread over the area. The period began around 500 BC,

Bronze Age Site

C.J.

with further invasions of the *Belgae* around 100 BC. The last named introduced trading, wheel-made pottery and the first coinage to Britain, and whilst there is plenty of Belgic occupation in east Berkshire, very little exists in the immediate area of Bray.

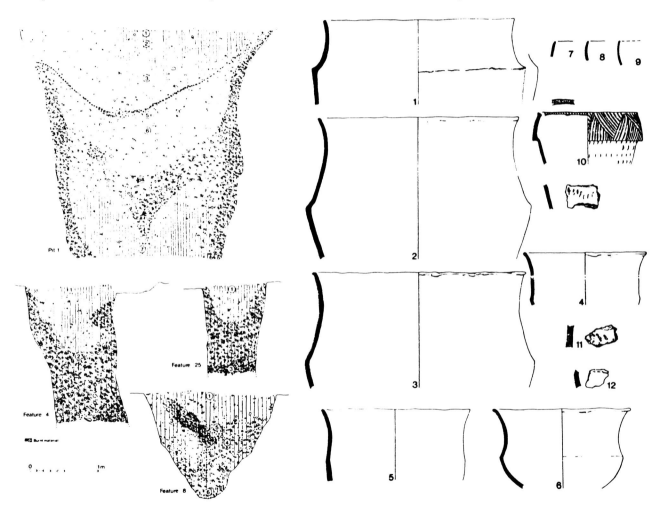

Neolithic Shafts and Pottery Excavated at Cannon Hill

CHAPTER III

Roman Bray

The first indication that there may have been a Romano-British settlement at Bray comes from the writings of Charles Julius Bertram, the son of a London silk dyer in 1758. In his book *De Situ Brittaniae*, which he purported to be the chronicle of the fourteenth century monk Richard of Cirencester, he clearly states that Bray was the river crossing on the main Roman road from London to Bath. The book, which at the time was heralded as an important historical publication, was later proved to be a very skilful forgery, and the information it contained about as genuine as Piltdown Man.

During the Romano-British period, Bray was in the territory of the *Atrebates* who had their capital at *Calleva Atrebratum*, the modern Silchester, some eight miles south of Reading. However, in the spurious map reproduced here, which was based on Bertram's information, the town of *Calleva* is shown to be at Streatley on the River Thames. The actual Thames crossing was at the Roman town of *Pontes*, modern Staines, but for some reason Bertram decided to delete this and substitute the town of *Bibrax* which he identified as Bray. Further to this he suggested that Bray was in the territory of the *Bibroci* tribe.

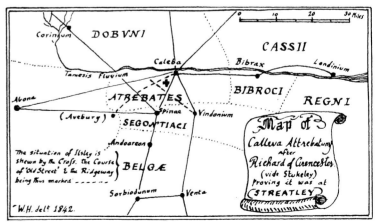

It was a hundred years before Bertram's book was proved to be a forgery, and during this period many mentioned Bray as a Roman station on the road from

London to Bath. Some gave the Roman name as *Bibracte* and some as *Bibrax*, but nobody to date seems to have appreciated that although the names are similar, they are in fact two separate towns in Roman Gaul. *Bibracte* was the principal town of the *Aeduii*, situated twelve miles west of Autun, whilst *Bibrax* was a town of the *Remi* tribe, a little north of the River Aisne, between Laon and Rheims. They both fell to Julius Caesar in 57BC. In his report on the *Conquest of Gaul*, Caesar mentions the *Bibroci* tribe, together with the *Segontiaci* and the *Cassi*, as being the three tribes that surrendered to him just prior to his defeat of Cassivellaunus at Wheathampstead in 54BC.

Despite Bertram's vivid imagination, excavations, field work and placenames suggest that Bray was a Romano-British settlement situated on the Thames near Water Oakley. The first indication of this was in the early nineteenth century when human remains and foundations of buildings were discovered in the gardens to the west of Down Place (now Bray Studios) at map reference SU918779. On another occasion coins of nine different emperors were found. Close by in a garden to the north west of Down Place coins and human remains were found at a depth of three feet.

Under normal circumstances most of these finds might have been dismissed as casual had it not been for extraction by the Hoveringham Gravel Company in a nearby field in 1970 (SU918781). Here a Roman site of considerable proportions was excavated, and proved to be a burial ground some 440 yards in width, which had a large number of inhumations and buried cremated remains stored in pottery vessels. Most of the skeletons uncovered showed signs of deformaties, with missing limbs and crippling arthritis in the bones. Some of the skulls had holes bored into the top, an ancient and usually fatal method of releasing pressure on the brain.

It was considered at the time that this might be the site of a primitive Roman hospital as amputations and other mutilations had taken place. Examination of the skeletons showed that nearly all the persons died at a very early age. Grave goods, indicating that the burials must have been pagan, date the interments to between AD320 and 400. Nearby, in the early fifth century some form of industrial activity had taken place on the site. In addition to this wooden posts were located on the river bank, which may have been a landing stage or flimsy bridge.

Cox Green Roman Villa.

Roman Baths at Cox Green Villa

Two years later, in the grounds of Down Place Cottage, some 60 skeletons were uncovered by floodlight in advance of a destructive bulldozer, and were assumed to be part of the same burial ground.

Burial grounds in Roman times were normally located outside of a settlement and therefore one should expect to find the living quarters nearby. Here we can probably rely on some placename evidence. In the Bray Court Rolls of 1336 the area next to Down Place is referred to as *Ereburghfeld Apud Ocle* translating as *Ere* (before), *burgh* (borough or town), *Apud Ocle* (near to Oakley), the whole being 'the field of the former town near Oakley'. Similarly in a survey of the Down Place estate dated 1747, a meadow is referred to as *Arbour Bridge* (former Town Bridge), which may be indicating a small river crossing near this point. Around 1800 Monkey Island Lane, which leads from Down Place to Bray, was also known as *Arbour Lane*, which might have been a subsidiary Roman road.

Some remains at the Bray end of Arbour Lane were noted in August 1795, when a writer in the *Gentleman's Magazine* recorded that 'a short piece of Roman highway was thought, some years ago, to have been discovered between the river and the east corner of Bray churchyard; and certain it is, that several Roman coins, together with fragments of armour and weapons, have been at different times ploughed up in the East Hay – a common field lying on the east side of Bray Town'. Also close to Arbour Lane the Bray Court Rolls records a *Braybury* (Bray Town) in 1362, and B*urypits*.

If Arbour Lane can be considered to be a Roman road, then an *agger* or raised bank behind houses at Fifield may be a continuation of it. At the northern end Arbour Lane runs in the direction of Braywick where a more plausible highway known as Alderman Silver's Roman Road was discovered last century. It can be traced as a well defined ridge across Braywick Park by the Nature Centre, through the graveyard passing close to Stafferton Lodge. At one time it was traceable to the railway embankment, but can be seen again in Kidwells Park, Maidenhead as it continues its course towards Cockmarsh at Cookham. The alignment would suggest a route linking the Roman settlements of Staines and High Wycombe.

Elsewhere in Bray Hundred finds of coins and other Romano-British artifacts indicate a well spread Roman occupation. Victorian antiquaries in the area tended to disregard most finds with the exception of coins, and therefore we find that before 1860 a Mr W H Woodwell had accumulated a collection of 118 coins all found in Bray Parish. A hoard of coins, hurriedly buried, was also found at Forest Farm, Oakley Green. An interesting solo find was an early Roman bow brooch from Mount Skipett, Moneyrow Green which can be dated to between AD50–80. This type of brooch works on the safety pin principle and was used mainly by women to fasten toga-like garments. Although this brooch seems to have been manufactured during the Romano-British period, it was probably made by native Britons. Quantities of late Iron Age pottery have been found on the surface at Mount Skipett, and a large circular earthwork of the same pre-Roman era has been identified from the air and encircles the summit of the hill.

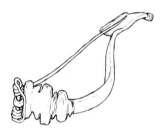

During the Romano-British period the Thames Valley was a relatively peaceful area mainly occupied by villa-farms producing wheat for a wider population. In the hundred of Bray two very good examples have been excavated. The most important of these was at Cox Green and was discovered from an aerial photograph when part of the Wessex Way estate was being built. It was fully excavated in 1959 and is now buried under a block of flats in Northumbria Road.

The Roman villa was shown to have 18 rooms at its final stage, with one outbuilding. There were four phases of building and occupation spanned over 200 years, after which the building was abandoned. The first building on the site was rectangular in plan, with one internal sub-division at the north western end. Evidence from the building indicated that the Period I building was of early Antonine date.

During Period II the villa was considerably extended and the original building sub-divided into 7 rooms, 3 of these being part of a new bath wing. A further six rooms were added, including a corridor, and the whole took on the classical shape of a winged-corridor villa. The bath wing at this stage consisted of six rooms, and a channelled *hypocaust*, to provide heating, was added to the Period I living room. Another room with a hearth and oven was assumed to be the kitchen.

A further four rooms were added in Period III, probably during the 3rd century AD. Two of these were to elaborate the baths wing, and another was identified as a forge. In Period IV, the bath wing was further altered some time after AD358. Finds from the site were considerable and included 110 coins, pottery, bronze and gold objects, beads and bones of domestic animals. The presence of iron slag was evidence that the metal was smelted in the vicinity of the villa.

Roman villas in east Berkshire tend to be a mile apart, indicating that each estate was probably quite large. Further features of Cox Green Villa complex occur in Altwood Bailey to the north of the railway line. In the back garden of three of the houses in the road Roman finds have come to light on different occasions. In 1948 a double kiln was excavated believed to have been used for the manufacture of roofing tiles for substantial Roman buildings. Numerous tiles with the characteristic markings of a specific tilemaker were found scattered around the site. Later, in 1961, a ditch containing large quantities of Romano-British pottery was located which was dated prior to AD150. In the 1980s a complete Roman well was excavated two gardens further up the road.

The other Roman villa was located just inside Bray Hundred at the top of Grenfell Road, Maidenhead, in 1886 by the antiquary James Rutland. Hurried excavations were carried out during which the furnace for the central heating system was

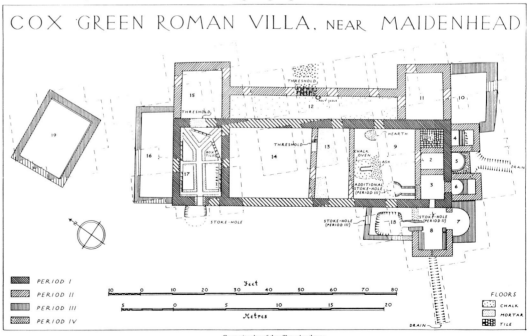

Composite plan of the villa and outhouse

revealed. In an adjacaent room was an underfloor *hypocaust* system with 27 *pilae*, or floor supports, still in situ. These rooms seem to be associated with the baths suite of the villa as a further two rooms nearby contained a bath and a bather's seat. In another area of the site Mr Rutland uncovered a kitchen midden with a lot of pottery and bones of most types of domestic animals that had been eaten as a source of food. This villa was not accurately dated but two coins of Tetricus (AD267–273) were found stratified in one of the rooms.

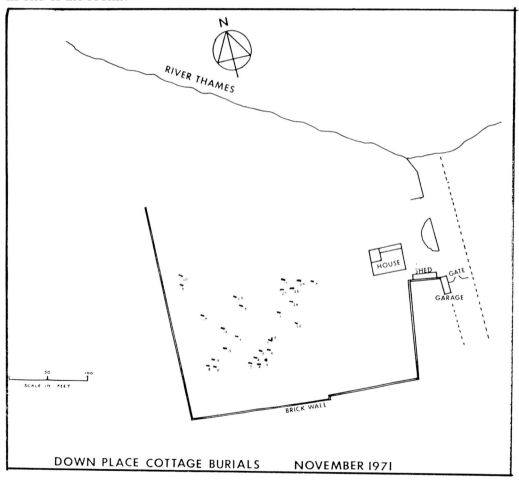

DOWN PLACE COTTAGE BURIALS   NOVEMBER 1971

CHAPTER IV

The Domesday Evidence

After the exodus of the Romans around AD400 the country lapsed into a period of history of which we know little and during which the legendary King Arthur is reputed to have reigned. The first King of Wessex, and the founder of the British Monarchy was Cerdic, the Saxon chieftain, who was crowned in the year 519. The fifth and sixth centuries AD were a period of disorder, war and battle, and it was some time before any sort of peace was established. Christianity came to Bray and the Thames Valley after AD634 when Bishop Birinus baptised the West Saxons, and by 675 Bray was part of the Provincia of Sonning and under ecclesiastical rule.

King Alfred was born in Wantage in 849 and in the year 851 the Anglo-Saxon Chronicles record that the Danes came up the Thames and were defeated by King Ethelwulf at the site of *Acleah*, south of the river. This is the Saxon name for Oakley (Oak Clearing) and therefore the battle could conceivably have taken place in Bray Hundred. The name *Batlyngmede* occurs in the Bray Court Rolls of 1368, and there is a tradition of a battle being fought on the unidentified Bray Downs. However, we cannot pinpoint the location with certainty.

The Chronicles tell us that the Danes made several raids up the Thames destroying villages as they went along, and seizing any valuables. In the years 870/1 the Danes took Reading for a short period but were driven away. To protect the Thames Alfred built the fort of *Sceaftesege* at Cookham in 886, but the Danes still persisted. In 1006 they went up-river as far as Wallingford and sacked the town, and continued their harassment for five years from 1009 to 1013 during which they took Oxford.

During this long period of instability Bray suffered along with most of the villages along the Thames. Saxon buildings, including churches where they existed, were burnt to the ground. There is little archaeological evidence of Bray during this troubled period but what there is will be mentioned in context. We can, however, learn a lot from the placenames in Bray Hundred which, with a few exceptions, come from the Anglo-Saxon language. As previously mentioned, the administrative *shires* and *hundreds* were set up at this time and were well in use by the time of the Norman invasion in 1066. With Edward the Confessor dead, and the Earl Harold slain at Hastings, the country was rife for takeover by William, Duke of Normandy.

After 20 years of his reign William I laid down plans for the Great Survey of England, which when completed became the Domesday Book. He instructed his barons and churchmen to prepare lists of their land-holdings together with information on resources and manpower. Accordingly a full list of names in each shire was prepared and presented to the king in 1086. From this information he hoped to keep a tighter reign on the annual taxes owed to him by his tenants.

The Domesday document was written in medieval Latin, and today remains the earliest available gazetteer of towns and villages in England, listed as boroughs and manors. The document is not perfect and has some discrepancies depending on the literacy of the clerks appointed to prepare it, but nevertheless provides a starting point for any historian studying the origins of a settlement. There are two entries in the Domesday Book for Bray listing the settlement as both *Brai* and *Bras*. The most important is the first and reads as follows:

'Land of the King in the Hundred of Bray. King Edward held it. 18 hides, they did not pay tax. Land for ... In lordship 3 ploughs; 56 villagers and 7 smallholders with 25 ploughs. 4 slaves; a church; 3 men-at-arms; meadow, 50 acres; woodland at 60 pigs.

The Domesday Book entries for Bray

Reinbald holds 1 hide which belongs to the church; he has 1 plough there. Value of the whole before 1066 £25; later £18; now £17.'

An analysis of this entry tells us that William I was holding the land in *desmesne*, or for his own use. Edward the Confessor held the land before the conquest in 1066, and until his death in January of that year. The size of the manor was 18 hides, which in modern terms is 2160 acres. The manor, apparently, did not pay tax, presumably because it was Crown property. The arable land is normally measured by the number of ploughs required for cultivation but this has been excluded. However, the ploughlands specifically reserved for the King is 3.

We then come to the labour force which includes 56 villagers, a class of peasant who holds the most land, and 7 smallholders who are further down the scale. Those listed are heads of households therefore the total is normally multiplied by four to calculate the actual population, which if we add the 4 slaves comes to 256 people. There were also 3 men-at-arms (*milites*), who were knights owing military service to their King. A church, much earlier than the present building is mentioned. As well as the arable land, for which the work force required 25 ploughs, there was also 50 acres of meadow and enough woodland to feed 60 pigs on acorns and beech mast for a whole year.

Of the total land Reinbald holds 1 hide (120 acres). This churchman is normally referred to as Reinbald the Priest, and his role at Bray was one of Rector, as indeed he was for at least 30 other churches. He is said to have been the King's Chancellor and Dean of the College of Prebendaries at Cirencester, and as such probably spent very little time at Bray. The entry mentions that Reinbald's hide of land belonged to the church, which is not referring to Bray Church, but rather to the church as an institution. The clue to this lies in the Latin wording which refers to Bray Church in the singular (*aeccla*) and to Reinbald's holding in the plural (*aecclae*). There was enough land for one plough in this holding.

The value of Bray manor is given in three stages. In the late Saxon period before the conquest it was worth £25. Later in the year 1070 when William I rewarded his knights the value had dropped to £18. Finally at the time of the Domesday Survey (c.1086), it had decreased to £17. The reason for the decline in value is not known, but in some cases it was due to damage caused by the Norman army on their advance across England.

An analysis of this Domesday entry tells us more about Bray as it was in the year 1086. The Rectory of Reinbald we know to be situated on Canon Hill at Braywick, as the name suggests. Reinbald's holding at Cookham is similarly situated at Can(n)on Court, although the name is now misspelt. Canon Hill in itself does not constitute 120 acres, but later documents suggest that the holding included the field known as *Queens Leaze* and the wood called *Rushenden*.

After Reinbald's death and when St Marys Abbey at Cirencester was consecrated, Henry I granted the church at Bray and the Rectory to the Abbey in 1133. This was confirmed by John and stayed in their possession until the dissolution in 1547 when Edward VI granted the lands to John King, Bishop of Oxford.

We know little of the ecclesiastical building at Canon Hill in the early period, the first description coming in 1340 when Abbot William is recorded as holding one messuage and 100 acres of land, together with four pieces of meadow with pastures, fisheries, rents and the tithe of all the meadows. In a survey of 1650 when the property had passed to the Marten family it was described as 'a fair Rectory or Parsonage House, being a new brick house with outhousing, yards and gardens enclosed with a brick wall plus arable ground of 50 acres in *Holyport Field*. The house owns the first crop in *Wickmeade* and the tithes of corn and hay'. At this time *Queens Leaze* was described as 66 acres of pasture ground and bounded by *Old Field* on the south and east, a common called *Wickfield* on the west and a meadow called *Foreleaze* in the north.

As to the main settlement of Bray as described in the Domesday Book, there is much evidence to suggest that it was not the village that we know today. Geographically speaking the settlement is badly sited on the flood plain of the Thames and even in the last hundred years has been subject to severe flooding prior to existing flood relief schemes. The Causeway running from Bray to Braywick is evidence for this and there is good reason for thinking that this public way is of some antiquity and may conceivably have been a route between the church and the rectory. In the eleventh century, before locks and weirs were built, the water in the Thames was high and capable of inflicting severe damage on flimsy Saxon buildings.

Although one would not expect early Norman buildings to have survived, there is no evidence as yet to prove that any building in the village pre-dates St Michael's Church, which was founded in 1293. Nor is there any proof that the church mentioned in Domesday Survey c.1086 was built on the same site, which after all is some distance from the Rectory at Canon Hill. The possibility that Bray village sprung up as a consequence of the present church being built is a point that cannot be overlooked.

There are two other points about the Domesday Book entry that support the hypothesis that the main settlement of Bray was located elsewhere in the Hundred. The first is the complete absence of mills and fisheries, which were two of the most important resources of any manor. All other Thames settlements, including Windsor, Clewer, Cookham and Hurley on the Berkshire bank are recorded as having these facilities. Manors without water mills were at a disadvantage as they had nowhere to mill their flour, and similarly those without fisheries could not rely on eel catches to supplement their diet. Normally only inland manors like Warfield and Winkfield were deficient of these facilities, and found it necessary to barter or come to some arrangement with an adjacent manor by the riverside. The earliest record of a mill at Bray was in 1206, when King John granted it to Jordan de London.

The second point concerns the presence of 3 men-at-arms or *milites*. These were not common foot soldiers, but rather Knights with their own contingent of men who owed service to their King. Such knights would be rewarded by their monarch with dwelling of manor house status and a small piece of land. It would seem that the King regarded the Hundred of Bray, being so close to Royal Windsor and adjacent to the Royal Forest, as a dormitory town where men of importance could live and commute to the Court on horseback in a very short time. This probably sums up the role of Bray and the reason why it was retained as a Royal manor. But where were the manor houses of the Knights? Certainly not in Bray village. Also the Domesday entry for Wallingford, then the county town of Berkshire, mentions that Miles Crispin, an important Norman Knight, held 1 acre in Bray and 11 dwellings there. In the context of the entry these dwellings were probably to house a contingent of guards on duty at Windsor Castle.

If we are to discount the present village as the main settlement of Bray Hundred in 1086 then we must look elsewhere for the manor described as *Brai*. If we accept the possibility that this name given to the Hundred is of Norman French origin, then it may have replaced an earlier Saxon name. All evidence then points to Holyport as the major settlement. Geographically sited centrally within Bray Hundred; it holds an ideal position as an administrative and market centre. Situated away from the Thames its resources would probably not include mills and fisheries, although these were available at nearby royal manors.

As far as Reinbald's rectory is concerned, its siting at Canon Hill is equidistant between Bray village and Holyport. We have no evidence of the earlier Saxon or Norman church but conceivably it may have stood adjacent to the rectory itself on higher ground. During the Medieval period the Hundred of Bray had no less than 14 manor houses, which will be discussed in detail in the next chapter. However, seven of these were located within Holyport with very little appended land, which indicates that they were probably the homes of the men-at-arms and other court officials.

The name Holyport is from the Anglo-Saxon and appears as *Horipord 1220, Holyport 1395, and Hollyport 1586*. The suffix *port*, especially when related to an inland town, denotes a market centre. Such centres were normally located at five mile intervals bearing in mind that market produce had to be transported on a horse-drawn vehicle, or in the case of animals driven by a herdsman on foot. In the case of Holyport, it was well positioned close to the Saxon road from Windsor to Reading, which is represented by the modern B3024. The antiquity of the road is evidenced by a number of ancient moats along its route notably at Wolf Lane, Dedworth; Mills Farm, Oakley Green; Fifield Manor and Foxleys Manor. Greens along the route, common land on which drovers could graze their animals were listed in a survey of 1608 as East Oakley Green (40 acres), Fifield Green (12), *Twychene* (Touchen End) (20), Stroud Green (50) and Moneyrow Green (30). Holyport Green was mentioned as 10 acres, but this presumably was the area of the market.

The earlier prefix *Hori* is thought to derive from the Saxon *Horrig* meaning 'muddy', making the whole 'muddy market town'. This rather unglamorous description seems to have been changed at a later date to *Holy*. This may well allude to local presence

Bray Causeway

41

Crutchfield Manor

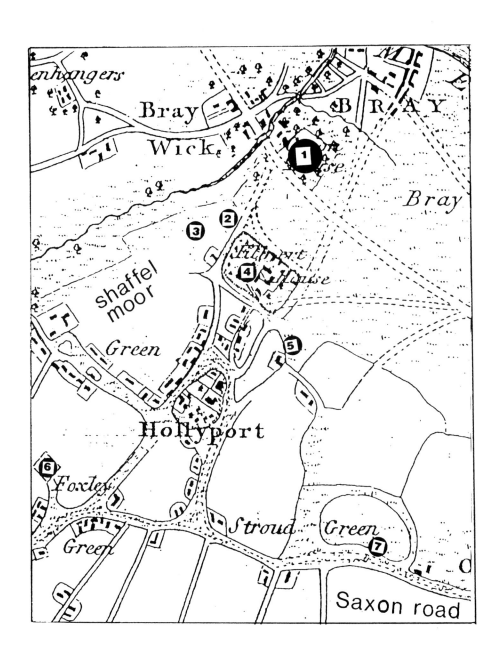

Location of Holyport Manors

Key   1. *Rectorial Manor*
           of Canons
       2. *Manor of Moors*
       3. *Cresswells*
       4. *Philiberts*
       5. *Manor of Stroud*
       6. *Foxleys*
       7. *Fifield*

of the canons of the Abbey of Cirencester, who during the early medieval period may have had control of the market centre and have been deriving an income from it.

The idea of ecclesiastical control of the market at Holyport is further enhanced when one considers other manors where Reinbald was rector of the church and held land. Apart from the 1 hide of land in Bray he held a further $1\frac{1}{2}$ hides in Cookham and the church of the manor, in which the Domesday Book mentions the existence of a 'new market'. Perhaps a better parallel with Holyport is the town of Milborne Port in Somerset, another inland *port* and market centre. In 1086 it is stated that 'in this manor there are 56 burgesses who pay 60 shillings with the market'. This was another royal manor that never paid tax like Bray, and in which Reinbald was rector of the church and held a further hide of land. Another similarity with Bray was the fact that Milborne Port was a pre-Conquest *minster*.

Archaeological evidence of Saxon occupation at Holyport comes from a site below Canon Hill on *Shaffelmoor Stream*. Here under a layer of peat preserved brushwood floors and wooden uprights of early buildings were excavated. Among the brushwood several pieces of grass marked pottery of the period were found. Pieces of wood sent off to the laboratory produced a middle radiocarbon date of AD753. During the conversion of Moor Farm barn nearer the village, similar finds of the same date were excavated below the floor.

The second Domesday entry for Bray is that of *Bras*, the translation reads as follows:

The manor lies in Beynhurst Hundred.

'Alwin, son of Chipping, holds BRAS from the King. Tovi held it from King Edward. Then for 2 hides, now for 1 hide. Land for 1 plough. It is there with 10 villagers who have 1 plough. A church. The value was 60 shillings now 30 shillings'.

This smaller manor with a population of 40 was held from the King, before and after the Conquest, by one of his tenants-in-chief, for some specific purpose. The strangest thing about it is the fact that whilst it is Bray, it is listed as being in the neighbouring Hundred of Beynhurst. This is perhaps explainable if we can equate *Bras* with the later manor of Crutchfield, or Lordlands situated at the top of Hawthorn Hill. For many years this has been designated as a deserted medieval village, which was wiped out around 1450 for the purpose of providing additional arable land. Evidence of the extent of the village comes from an archaeological evaluation in 1991, and an aerial photograph which outlines the settlement.

Crutchfield was listed as *Kerchesfeld* in 1185, and is mentioned as being 1 hide in size when held by Henry Lovell in 1272, which is the equivalent to the Domesday site of *Bras*. LIke all *field* names in the area, it was originally a clearing in the Royal Forest of Windsor and therefore much under the eyes of the monarch. The prefix *Kerches* probably alludes to a cross made on an oak tree to delineate the boundary between the hundreds of Bray and Beynhurst. For 500 years this boundary was the cause of a dispute.

Shaffelmoor Stream

In the Close Rolls of 1286 we find the entry reading 'Cruchefend was formerly the Kings *vaccaria* (dairy and cow shed) and that it is in *Le Fryth* (the forest). For 200 years (ie from Domesday) and more the rectors of Bray Church received the offerings and all manners of the tithes then arising'. In the same year a survey of the Parish of Bray in connection with a dispute between the Dean of Salisbury and the Abbot of Cirencester about the tithes of Crutchfield, which the Dean claimed on the grounds that Crutchfield was in the Frith, and that all the forest tithes had been granted to him by charter. It was decided on this occasion that Crutchfield belonged to the Parish of Bray.

This dispute over the boundary between Bray and Beynhurst continued until December 1807 when it was settled after a meeting in the vestry of Bray Church. In the early stages a Red Stone was placed on the border, being more substantial than a cross on a tree, and the site of this still perpetuates in the name of Redstone Farm at Hawthorn Hill. The dispute, however, probably explains why the settlement of *Bras* was listed as being in Beynhurst Hundred at Domesday.

The mention of a church at *Bras*, which cannot be accounted for as a site for a present day church, still remains a mystery, but perhaps as the Abbot of Cirencester was benefitting from the tithes he may have set up a small chapel for the 40 villagers known to be working at this outpost in Bray.

CHAPTER V
Sub-Infeudation and the Manor Houses

Throughout the medieval period and until its final abolishment in 1661, the *feudal* system was in operation in England. This system was probably in operation during the time of Edward the Confessor, but was certainly adopted by the Normans after the Conquest. William I worked on the principle that society was a pyramid, where each man was tied to his superior and ultimately to the King. All lands belonged to the monarch, but William granted them in the year 1070 to tenants-in-chief or major monasteries in return for specific services. Either way the King benefitted from taxation or in kind.

The unit within the *feudal* system was the *manor,* which describes a self-sufficient estate usually with arable and grazing lands, mills and fisheries. The manor had its own labour force, which was made up of free and unfree tenants, who were responsible to the headman or *reeve.* The reeve in turn was responsible to the *bailiff,* who responded to the *tenant-in-chief* or lord of the manor. Each manor had its own *manor house,* often moated, in which the lord or his representative lived. Part of the estate, termed the *demesne,* was reserved for the personal requirements of the lord's household and was worked for him by his unfree tenants. A majority of manors had their own courts, in which the lord dealt with breaches of the regulations for husbandry, tenurial matters and minor misdemeanours.

The manor of Bray belonged to the ancient demesne of the Crown, and was usually let for farming to a succession of wardens. For a long period Bray was part of the Queen's dowry, the earliest recorded being Queen Eleanor in 1193. It was again granted in Dower to Queen Margaret of France who was patron of the church in 1293, and then to Isabel in 1327 for her services in the matter of the treaty with France. Between 1331 and 1360 it was held by Queen Philippa, and was subsequently granted to Anne of Bohemia. Henry IV, however, gave it to his son Humphrey, Duke of Gloucester but it reverted to the Crown in 1447. Other Tudor queens with which the manor was associated were Elizabeth, queen of Edward IV, Catherine of Aragon, Anne Boleyn and Jane Seymour. During the Civil War it was taken over by the Parliamentary Commissioners in 1649, and was again restored to the Crown. After the Restoration it remained Crown property until 1818 when it was purchased by Pascoe Grenfell of Taplow Court.

In so much that the manor of Bray was a Royal Demesne, there was probably no manor house in which the lord lived, as it was administered from Windsor. However, the manor courthouse was situated on the site of Braywick School and was described in 1650 as 'all that messuage and tenement called the Court House, lying and being within the Parish of Bray, containing 2 rooms, with a parcel of land thereunto adjoining, containing by estimation one acre and a half.' The building was mentioned in 1454 when it was said that 'the tithingmen of Braywick presented that the fences around the Courthouse were broken and out of repair'. Common lands in the manor included those mentioned in the previous chapter with common woods at Bray Naits (250 acres), Bray Woods (200 acres) and Altwood (220 acres). The field known as *Queen's Leaze* or Lease, derives its name from the fact that parishioners paid a nominal rent to the Queen, which proceeds were devoted to the repairs of the church. The last lease on this property expired in 1821, when 72 acres of land were sold by auction at the Sun Inn, Maidenhead.

In the fourteenth century the revenue of the manor of Bray was derived from two principal sources. The first was from feudal obligations including licenses for contracts, heriots, reliefs, wardships, fines and the proceeds of the courts, and the second was the various rents issuing from the demesne e.g. pannage, agistments, and fisheries.

By the year 1166 many of the original manors were broken up by sub-infeudation into several smaller manors held by many of the wealthy local gentry. Bray itself was remarkable in that it had 14 such manors during the medieval period, although many

Old Philiberts

C.J.

Foxleys Moat

were merely manor houses for officers who served the King, with very little land attached as per the 7 that were located in the Holyport area. Many of these buildings still exist today, albeit as farms and private houses which have been rebuilt over the centuries.

The manor of *Philberds* or *Cresswell* belonged in 1208 to Roger de St Philibert, who granted it in that year to his brother Hugh. In 1276 the manor was charged with providing the King with one bushel of wine. In 1317 John de St Philibert obtained free warren in Cresswell and the manor stayed with the family until 1352 when it was sold to Edward III. The King granted it to St Georges Chapel, Windsor who held it until 1649 when the Parliamentary Commissioners sold it to Edward Curle and Richard Spencer. After the Restoration the Dean and Canons of Windsor recovered their land, and held the manor until 1860 when it was bought by Charles Pascoe Grenfell. The house of Philberts has now been demolished but the moat which surrounded the building can still be seen in the field at the end of Holyport Street. The name Cresswell still perpetuates as a farmhouse.

The manor of *Cruchfield* alias *Lordslands* or *Hawthorne*, was discussed in association with the Domesday manor at *Bras*, when it was a dairy farm belonging to the royal manor of Bray. Henry de Baggesite was in possession of it between 1186 and 1217, and his son Geoffrey gave the estate to the Queen's cook, Henry Lovel in 1250. John de Cruchfield, who presumably took his name from the estate, succeeded to the property in 1333 and kept it in the family until 1525. It then passed to William Hyde, who sold it in 1608 to William Goddard from the Fishmongers Company and the income it derived was used to support Jesus Hospital, which he had founded in Bray. The present Crutchfield House probably dates to around 1800.

The manor at *Foxleys* was known as *Pokemere* in the 13th century, and seems to have been formed from various holdings in Bray acquired in the 14th century by Sir John de Foxley from his father Sir Thomas, who was constable of Windsor Castle. In 1321 Sir John was granted license to make a deer park there which in 1344 had the fence broken down and the deer stolen. Before 1266 Henry Wade owned some of the Pokemere land and obtained an extra 30 acres from Geoffrey de Picheford, constable of Windsor Castle in 1273. Another Sir Thomas de Foxley was also appointed constable

Old Hendons

Lillibrooke Manor

53

in 1330 and died in 1361 leaving the estate to his son John. This Sir John married Maud Brocas, a local lady whose family can be associated with the riverside meadow at Eton. Their son-in-law Robert Bullock links with the area known as Bullock's Hatch or East Oakley. In 1498 the manor passed to Sir Reynold Bray and then to Lord Sandys in 1510. The manor house was burnt down some time before 1750, and today the site is represented by a well kept quadrangular moat of 350 yards in circumference.

The history of the fine half-timbered manor house known as *Ockwells* will be discussed later but the earlier history of the manor of *Ockholt* alias *Norreys* can be recorded here. The name translating as 'Oak Wood' probably refers to a hunting lodge in the Forest of Windsor. The manor seems to have originated as a *purpestre* taken into cultivation between 1251 and 1259 and granted before 1284 to Richard le Norreys. He is recorded as paying threepence for the pastorage of his cattle in the *Frith* (thicket) near Ockwells in 1334. In 1447 John Norreys is recorded as the Steward of the manors of Bray & Cookham and his third wife, who died in 1495, as Margaret, Duchess of Norfolk.

The Hall of Ockwells.

The first mention of the manor at *Lowbrook* occurs in 1376 when Thomas de Lollebrooke appeared in court to exhibit his title for it. The names *Lillibrooke* or *Lollibrooke* appear to have been the original titles for the manor and the present farmhouse is known as Lillibrooke Manor. Whilst this may have occurred as a later manor in Bray, the family had previously acquired lands in Cookham as early as 1292 when Walter de Lillebrok obtained a messuage, lands and rent from Joan

Ockwells Manor

Moor Farmhouse

de la Lane of Elington (Maidenhead). In 1412 the manor passed into the hands of the Martyn family of Athelhampton, Dorset who held it until 1525 when Christopher Martyn died. It then passed to the Englefield family until 1656 when it was purchased by Henry Partridge, a citizen and cooper of London. Eventually it was bought in 1861 by Charles Pascoe Grenfell with other manors in the area.

The manor of *Hyndens* or *Hendons* exists today as *Lyndens Manor* in Holyport. In 1296 it was known as *John de Brayes* place, when the Bray family were living there. John de Bray, from whom it took its earlier name, held it until his death in 1333, and in the following year Walter de Bray died seised of the lands in Bray formerly held by John de Hyndon. The Hyndon family held the manor between 1340 and 1445 when it was granted to John Norreys by Humphrey, Duke of Gloucester. In 1609 Frances, Lord Norreys sold the estate to Sir Thomas Bodley who bequeathed it in 1612 to the University of Oxford for the support of the library there which bears his name. The old manor house of Hendons was in the main taken down in 1846, and was originally surrounded by a moat which was filled in about the same time. The house contained a chapel, with a fine old group of chimney shafts said to have been erected in 1570.

The manor of *Mores* or *Moors* perpetuates today in Moor Farm, a part of the farmhouse of which probably represented the manor house. The name has undoubtedly been taken from the marshy area adjoining Braywick known as the *Shaffelmoor* or *Shortfordmoor* (1270). The first member of the family was mentioned in 1288 as John atte More (John at the moor), when he was one of the principal tenants at an inquest concerning Bray Mill. Members of the More family, who also had land in Cookham continued to hold the manor until 1540 when Thomas More was the tenant. In 1495 it was described as a messuage with 80 acres of pasture and the siting of its land can be determined from a note in 1455 that 'William Barnard, tithingman of Braywick, presented that fences between the land called *Moris* and the road leading from Braywick to Maidenhead ought to be repaired'. By 1550 it seems to have passed into the hands of Lord Norreys and then eventually in 1855 to John Coney of Braywick Grove.

The manor of *Ives* is interesting in that the manor house stood adjacent to Maidenhead High Street on the site of the Town Hall, with lands stretching down to Forelease Road. In its later life it was known as both Ives Place and St Ives Place. The 'saint' prefix is a

Shoppenhangers Manor

Stroud Farmhouse

misnomer, being added in 1870 by William Wilberforce, son of the man who abolished slavery. The building itself was demolished in the 1960s, and Queen Anne House in the Broadway is believed to be a farmhouse belonging to the manor.

The family had been settled in the parish from at least 1248 when Thomas *Yve* occurs in a local charter. The manor only stayed in the *Ive* family for a short time, and by 1376 it was in the hands of Eleanor Brid. In the following year it was bought by William Montagu, Earl of Salisbury who granted it to the Abbey at Bisham. The religious house held the manor until the dissolution, when Henry VIII granted it to Anne of Cleves in 1541 as part of a divorce settlement. By 1559 the manor was in lay hands and had numerous owners, including Penyston Portlock Powney, who died there in 1794.

The present manor house of *Shoppenhangers* was built in 1915 and will be discussed later. However, the manor itself dates back to 1204 when Roger de Shobenhangre is mentioned as a tenant. The name derives from the Anglo-Saxon *Scoben Hangan*, meaning the 'hanging woods', which describes the area where it is situated. The family held the manor until 1362, when it seems to have passed to the Crutchfields and then in the early 17th century to the Winch family. The estate was purchased by Pascoe Grenfell in 1801, and was passed on to his son, Charles Pascoe Grenfell.

Stroud Farm is the site of the original manor of *Stroud, Staverton* or *Shiplake*, and the building itself has 14th century roof timbers. The earliest name of the manor seems to be Stroud, although the earliest recorded resident is Robertus de Shiplake in 1293. In 1373, Thomas Puttenham, vicar of Bisham, did homage for Roberts' lands in Bray, but by 1422 it had passed into the Staverton family. William Staverton was one of the surveyors of the pontage for Maidenhead Bridge in 1400, and was killed in the following year by evil doers. It remained with the Staverton family until 1524 when it passed to the Loggins family by marriage. It then passed to the Blagrave estate at Bulmarsh Court, Surrey, from whom it was purchased by Archbishop Laud, who bequeathed it in 1640 to the Corporation of Reading. Stafferton Lodge on the Braywick Road has connections with this manor.

The rectorial manor of *Canon Hill* must be listed among the medieval manors but has been covered in an earlier chapter. The reported manor of *Winkles*, which cannot be

Fifield Manor

C.J

61

accounted for among existing manor houses, seems to have been a collection of various holdings acquired in the 14th century by one owner, John Brocas. One of these had been granted by Henry III to Simon Hartaud in 1253 and passed from his descendent Nicholas Hartaud to John Brocas about 1337. The rest were chiefly purpestres taken into cultivation towards the end of the 13th century and rented to various holders by Geoffrey de Pycheford and his successors, wardens of Bray.

Fifield House, a reputed manor was anciently the property and residence of a branch of the Norreys family of Ockwells, and probably inherited by them from the Fowlers. John Fowler, of Fifield, who died in 1479 married Agnes, daughter of William Norreys. Fifield House was afterwards in the family of Winch, from whom it descended to the Micklems. The house is not standing today.

Several of the Bray manors were purchased by the Grenfell family of Taplow Court. Pascoe Grenfell bought Shoppenhangers in 1801, and his son Charles Pascoe Grenfell purchased Philberds in 1860, and Ockwells and Lowbrooks in 1861.

Ives House

CHAPTER VI
Bray Village and Braywick

The village of Bray as we see it today, is small and compact and basically comprises a church, a chauntry chapel, 5 inns or public houses, a group of almshouses and a variety of scheduled dwellings. It has a quaint and attractive appeal, and unlike Cookham, lacks the parade of shops and commercialities. The church, as one might expect, is by far the oldest building in the village, and replaced an even earlier place of worship which may or may not have been on the same site.

The church of St Michael was built in the year 1293 and replaced an earlier Saxon or Norman building. We can be certain about the date as the Bray Court Rolls record that Queen Margaret, second wife to Edward I, was made patron of the church soon after her marriage to the King, and had difficulty in extracting payment for the building from her tenants, as the following extract reveals:

'It was given to be understood by the wardens of the fabric of the Church at Bray, of which our Lady the Queen is patron, that an assessment was formerly made to the aforesaid fabric by the consent of the whole community of parishioners, and that very many tenants of our Lady the Queen who to the said fabric were assessed, refuse to pay that assessment by which the said work of the church aforesaid is delayed. And because our lady the Queen is bound to maintain the said church by reason of the

Anno 21 Edw. I. (1293). " Datū est intelligi p ̄pcuratores fabrice ectie de Braye de qua dña Regina patronᴀ est qd qued' assessio nup p asseñs' cōitatis ōium poc̄ fcā fuit ad fabricā p⁹dc̄m & qd q̇mplures tenentes dne R⁰ q̄ᶦ ad dc̄ām fabric' assessi fu⁹ūt, illā assessionē solu⁹e recusant p qd dc̄m op' ectiᴇ p⁹dc̄e tardat˜et q' dña Regina tene˜ iuvare mainctenere dc̄am ectiam rŏne patronatus p⁹dc̄e Idō p' est bedello qd diligent' eat cū dc̄is ̄pcurat' ad levand' dc̄ām assessiōne de hiis qui solu⁹e eam recusaut."

patronage aforesaid, wherefore it is commanded to the beadle that he go with the said church wardens diligently to raise the said assessment from those who refuse to pay it.'

As with many of the parish churches in the area, St Michael's has been renovated over the years and suffered the usual Victorian restoration. The church comprises a south tower, nave, north and south aisles, chancel and north and south chapels. Existing remains of the original building include the nave arches with a portion of the chancel and the west end of the church including the nave door. The north wall as far as the chapel of St Nicholas also dates from this period together with the basement of the upper chancel and the piscina.

The next addition seems to be the tower added in c.1400 with a square stair turret slightly projecting. Of the two chapels at the east end of the church the Chapel of All Saints was formerly detached from the south aisle has a piscina in the middle of the south wall. The ancient wooden porch on the south side of the chapel was removed in 1840, and the chapel restored by Edward Palmer of Canon Hill in 1860. The Chapel of St Nicholas, on the north east corner, seems to have been reconstructed about 1530.

Although the church wardens' accounts record several renovations during the 17th century, the main period of restoration took place between 1859 and 1862 under the supervision of T H Wyatt and when the Rev. Austin Leigh was vicar. In 1859 the gallery was removed and the chancel restored. Arches were built at the west of the chancel and chapels, and thick masses of masonry were removed from the entrances to the chapels. The south chapel was restored in 1860, the style being altered from late to early Perpendicular. Then the nave and aisles were restored, the north wall was rebuilt, the pillars were removed, the west entrance was re-opened, and the roof raised.

The first recorded incumbent of the church was Henry de Chilbolton who was appointed in 1301, but perhaps the most famous Vicar of Bray is the one about whom the famous ballad was written and is described by Fuller in his book of *Worthies* published in 1662. He tells the story as follows:

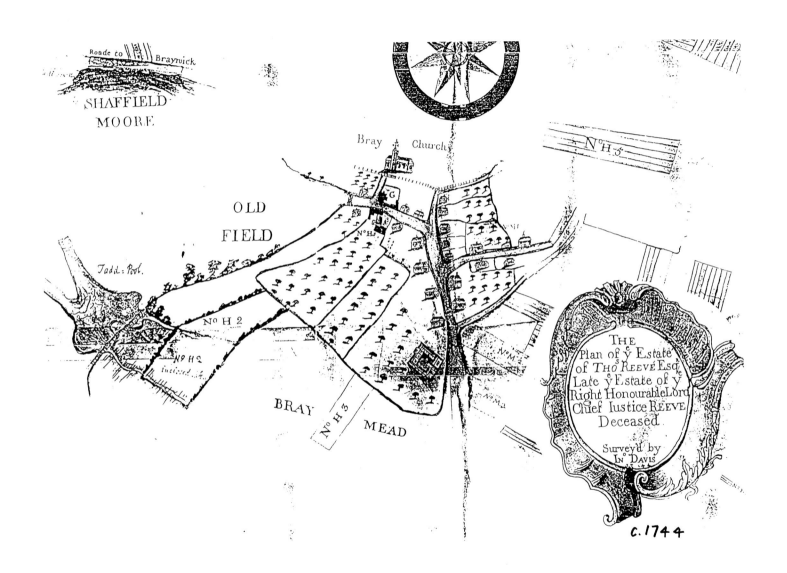

Roude to Braywick

SHAFFIELD
MOORE

Bray   Church

Nᵒ H 3

OLD

FIELD

Tadd=Pool.

Nᵒ H 2

Nᵒ H 2
Inclosed

Nᵒ H 2

G

Nᵒ H 3

Nᵒ M

Nᵒ M 2

Nᵒ M 3

BRAY   MEAD

THE
Plan of yᵉ Estate
of Thoˢ Reeve Esqᵉ
Late yᵉ Estate of yᵉ
Right Honourable Lord
Chief Iustice Reeve
Deceased

Surveyd by
Iⁿ Davis

c. 1744

65

St. Michaels Church

St. Michaels Church as it was in 1760

'The vivacious vicar hereof, living under King Henry the Eighth, Edward the Sixth, Queen Mary and Queen Elizabeth, was first a Papist, then a Protestant, then a Papist, then a Protestant again. He had seen some martyrs burnt two miles off at Windsor, and found this fire too hot for his tender temper. The vicar being taxed by one for being a turncoat, and inconsistent changeling, 'Not so,' said he, 'for I always kept my principle, which is this – to live and die the Vicar of Bray'. Such many nowadays, who though they cannot turn the wind, will turn their mills, and set them so, wheresoever it bloweth, their grist shall certainly be grinded.'

The vicar concerned, who is described as a systematic turncoat because he changed his religious beliefs according to which monarch was on the throne, is difficult to identify. According to Fuller, he would have needed to be the incumbent from 1533 when Henry VIII broke with Rome until at least 1558 when Elizabeth came to the throne. No vicar seems to have achieved this but the contenders are Symon Symonds (1523–47), William Stafferton (1547–54) and Simon Aleyn who is recorded as dying in 1563.The latter is the popular choice, although Aleyn could only have been vicar during the reigns of Mary and Elizabeth. On the other hand the other two contenders also only lived through the reigns of two monarchs. At present the identity of the famous vicar must remain an enigma, but no doubt Bray will bask in the reflected glory of the ballad which was written some time between 1714 and 1727.

On the north side of the churchyard stands the ancient chauntry chapel dedicated to the Blessed Virgin Mary and built around the same time as the church, as Thomas atte Grenedoune is recorded as chaplain in 1297. This rectangular building was probably originally founded to pray for the departed soul of Queen Eleanor, the first wife of Edward I, who died in 1290. A list of chaplains and clerks associated with the chapel are recorded in the Bray Court Rolls, and in some cases they appeared to have had a dual role. Several of the clerks also officiated at the Hermitage Chapel of St Leonard, which was situated in Windsor Forest and equates with the lost Domesday site of *Losfelle*. It would seem that the chapel was closed down at the Dissolution in 1547 at which time the last chaplain William Staverton took over as vicar of the church.

For a long period the chauntry became a drying and storage place for fishermen's nets as evidenced by hooks embedded in the ceiling. Many burials had taken place within the building and the church accounts record that the memorial stones were removed in 1631, presumably because of the change of use. In 1683 William Cherry of Shottesbrooke converted the building into a parish schoolroom and library and made an allowance of £26 per year for schoolmasters wages. He enclosed the east end with panelling and made a cottage for the schoolmaster from the two floors. The school continued until the opening of Braywick School in 1819, after which the building was used for meetings. The Chapel was refurbished in 1959 after which it was renamed St Michael's Hall. At one time a shed adjacent to the hall housed the Bray fire engine which was presented to the village in 1737 by Lady Colleraine of Canon Hill.

There is an interesting piece of stonework built into the side wall of the old chapel, which has probably been rescued from an earlier Saxon or Norman church in Bray. The carving represents a hound, and this is often associated with an old legend which maintains that the original site chosen for the church was at *Builders Well*, close to the Fifield crossroads. The story goes that whilst the foundations of the building were being laid during the day, the same were being moved each night by the 'powers of darkness' to the present church site. In the end the frustrated builders gave up and commenced work in Bray village. This legend may have some plausable relevance as the site, which is probably a natural spring, is recorded as early as 1424 as *Bylderes Well*.

Carving of a hound on the wall of St. Mary Chauntry

Another building associated with the church is the Lych Gate, where it was traditional for the clergy to meet a coffin at a funeral. Carved into one of the timbers is the date of 1448, which, strangely enough, is in arabic numerals. Although termed 'arabic' the origin of the numerals is thought to be Indian, and these were apparently used to some extent in medieval times. The accommodation above the Lych

C.J.

Lych Gate

69

St. Mary Chauntry

Gate was at one time the home of the chauntry priest, and during its lifetime has been both a dwelling and a public house. In a deed of 1763 it is referred to as 'a public house commonly called or known as The Six Bells, and is being rented to John Stokes by Richard Tonson for one year in payment of one peppercorn'. The building was purchased by Rev Walter Levett in 1839, and presented to the parish by him in 1853, as a residence for two poor persons.

Arabic numerals on Lych Gate

To the west of the church is Chauntry House Hotel which was erected in 1753. However, there was an earlier building on the site called *The Chauntrye* recorded in the Bray Court Rolls in 1504 when it was stated that 'Hugo Tanner presented that Thomas Horne kept a *Tenys-play* (tennis court) at his house called Le Chauntrye. Wherefore he is ordered to abolish the same, under penalty of three shillings and fourpence'. It was also presented that Thomas had a *bowlyngale* (bowling alley) within his premise which had to be dispensed with. In 1597 it was the property of Henry Norris. In 1705 Louis Grove, a cloth worker of Bray leased the premises to John Langutt.

In 1753 this older building seems to have been demolished and the present one built on the site. From the outset it was probably a workhouse, infirmary and jail. A Miss Heath reporting in 1908 described the cellars as containing two cells with gratings and spiked iron doors and some long slate slabs on which the dead were laid out. In the kitchen was a long and solid wooden table used by the workhouse inmates for meals. Her father, Mr Heath, whilst digging in the back garden, located a number of human bones but foul play was not suspected. It probably ceased to be a workhouse by 1834 when the Poor Law Amendment Act was issued and is reported in 1861 to be the property of a Mrs Williams. It remained in private hands after that date and was eventually turned into flats and then an hotel.

Of the five inns in the village, the Hinds' Head is probably the oldest. As the building stands now it appears to be late 15th century, and with its position adjacent to the church it may well have been an early hospice associated with the Abbey of Cirencester as is Churchgate House at Cookham. Originally it was a timber-famed hall house, but seems to have been divided into two cottages. The right hand corner cottage was at

Chauntry House Hotel

Hinds Head

some unrecorded date turned into a small inn and certainly by 1893 when it was held by the brewers Neville Reid & Co.

The hotel and restaurant started in 1928 when Kitty Henry, sometimes known as 'Champagne Kitty', a night club owner in London, purchased the small inn and the adjoining Vine cottage. By knocking them together, and then buying No. 5 Church Street, she had a large enough property for her requirements. She engaged Barry Neame as hotel manager who put the Hind's Head on the map by attracting royalty from Windsor, and film stars from Bray Studios. On one occasion The Queen and Prince Philip entertained five other Queens and foreign dignitaries to lunch in the hotel.

The Ringers public house, lying adjacent to the Hind's Head, started life as a 16th century cottage. The various owners of this cottage are known from 1744, but it may not have been a beerhouse until 1896 when it passed into the hands of John Fuller the brewer. The Crown in the High Street dates from the same period and again started as two cottages. This inn has obviously been a hostelry for some time as it was known in the time of George II (1727–60) to supply beer to cottages in the area. And if we are to believe that Charles II often called into the Crown for a drink when visiting Nell Gwynn at Holyport this could take it back one century earlier.

The Waterside Inn which stands by the site of the ferry, has only been called that since 1948. The previous inn of that name stood on the opposite side of Ferry Road where Linum Cottage now stands. In the 18th century it was a private house called 'Charlese', but by 1893 it was the George Inn. In the 1920s it had a reputation of being a rowdy establishment which attracted weekenders. In contrast, the Albion in Old Mill Lane was built around 1850 by a Mr Mickley, and housed the bargees who brought coal and timber to the wharf at Bray.

There are numerous listed buildings in the village which date back to the 15th and 16th centuries. It is not appropriate to mention all of them but one that stands out in the High Street is The Old Dutch House, close by the War memorial. This was originally called 'Dormer Cottage' and was a farmhouse with pond. It took its present name from a Miss Holland, who had the nickname of 'Old Dutch'. Betty Balfour, a stage actress, also lived in the house.

The Ringers

The Waterside

The Old Dutch House

C.J.

Jesus Hospital

The other building in the village that merits attention is that of Jesus Hospital, a grade I listed building built entirely of early brick with stone dressings. It was formerly a group of 40 almshouses built around a quadrangle with a chaplains house and gardens. It was founded in the year 1609 by William Goddard of the Fishmongers Company of London to house 40 poor people, but he had obviously been planning for some time as the Bray Court Rolls record that he purchased numerous properties in Bray between the years 1595 and 1598 with which to endow the property. Unfortunately Goddard died in the foundation year but left instructions for the ultimate construction which was completed in 1628. A memorial to William Goddard can be seen in the church. Above the attractive entrance facade were the former chaplains rooms, with a window on each side of a segmental leaded niche which contains a figure of William Goddard. Below the niche is a stone tablet with the date 1627 and an inscription. Today there are only 16 almshouses.

Some half a mile from the village at the other end of the causeway is the smaller settlement of Braywick. In 1336 it was known as *Wyke*, the prefix Bray being applied about 1450. This name is fairly common in England and derives from the Latin word *vicus* (a settlement) or the Anglo-Saxon *wic* basically meaning a collection of buildings, or a single building for a specific purpose, often a farm or a dairy. *Wick* settlements were often a satellite community of a larger place as in the case of Bray. *Wicks* are also in close proximity to Roman roads which also appears to be the case at Braywick.

Cottages in Hibbert Road

Wyke was one of the ancient tithings of Bray parish and there are many mentions of the tithingman in the Court Rolls. One amusing example occurred in 1617 when '*Robert Malden, tithingman, presented that Alice Smythgate of Braywick is a babbler and has an unruly tongue, wherefore the said Alice is commanded to refrain herself by the Feast of St Edmund under penalty of forty shillings and bodily punishment*'.

At the end of the Bray Causeway there is an interesting row of five cottages which were originally built in 1780 and extended in 1870. On the appropriate side of Hibbert Road is the Braywick School, once the site of the old courthouse. The site on the corner where the Nature Centre now stands was once the gardens of Braywick Lodge, an 18th century mansion which was the home of the Hibbert family. In 1857 John Hibbert gave £1000 to the funds of Jesus Hospital and in 1873 provided the money to build St Mark's Church in Maidenhead. The house no longer exists, but the gardens have been made into a public park.

There are few buildings of interest on the Braywick Road. The Stag & Hounds became a public house before 1845 but was quoted in 1814 as being 'a dwelling house and carpenters shop owned by Mr William Strugnell'. At one time there was a slaughter house situated behind the buildings. The mansion opposite now known as Braywick House was originally Braywick Grove and was built by Sir William Paule in 1675. This house has held numerous owners and has been preserved in style.

The final residence worthy of mention is Canon Hill House, now demolished, which stood on the site of The

Canon Hill House

The garden steps of Braywick Lodge

Binghams. Mention has previously been made of this area as Reinbald's holding and the site of the Rectory. The final house on the site, which was demolished in 1973, appears to have started life in the 17th century. In 1750 the famous Adam brothers made additions to the house including fireplaces, ceilings and mouldings. The house had a chapel built into the interior.

Braywick House

CHAPTER VII

The Oakleys

The Oakleys are a group of settlements comprising Oakley Green, East Oakley and Water Oakley. The name is derived from the Old English 'ac-leah' which translates as a clearing in an oak wood. In the Bray context the oak wood refers to Windsor Forest, a vast area laid out by the Norman Kings for hunting purposes. On the Norden map of 1607 the perimeter of this Forest is shown to be 77 miles, although 300 years earlier it had been even larger. Today, the remaining portions make up what we know as Windsor Great Park.

The oak was the main tree in Windsor Forest, and there are many records of trees being cut down and transported to Windsor and Maidenhead for repairs to the wooden bridges crossing the Thames. Other local placenames in the area which have connections with the oak forest are Ockholt or Ockwells Manor and Oakingham, the older name for Wokingham.

Oakley Green, which is probably the oldest settlement, is likely to have evolved as an assart or clearing hewn out of the Forest. As the village extended towards Windsor, East Oakley came into existence, and then finally Water Oakley, being that part of the settlement located along the banks of the river. The whole complex may well have been in existence in Anglo-Saxon times.

In the section of Norden's map reproduced here it can be seen that a large portion of Bray including the Oakleys belonged to the estate of New Lodge, the main house of which is situated on the Bray/Winkfield border. Its original area is not known, but a sale catalogue of 1916 records the estate as 3,736 acres with over 20 farms and numerous inns and cottages. A majority of the land came from Windsor Forest and the adjacent *Braywood*, listed in 1608 as 200 acres in size. The whole tract of land as far as the river Thames was designated as *New Lodge Walke* in medieval times.

The present New Lodge was erected in 1857 by Jean Sylvain Van de Weyer, the Belgian Minister to the English Court and Parliament. It was built in Jacobean style and replaced an earlier building of the same name which is shown on Norden's map. The name is a misnomer, and the prefix 'New' probably just indicates that it was the latest of the many lodges built in Windsor Forest. The Duke of Cumberland is said to have resided there in 1751 when he was Ranger of the Forest.

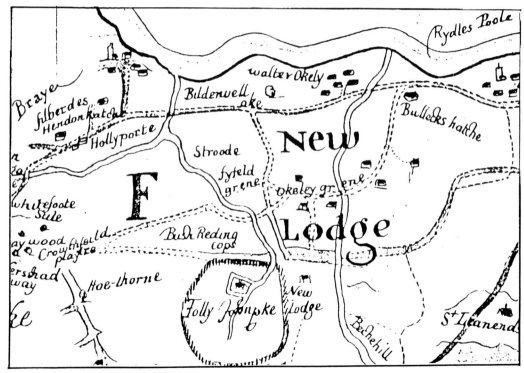

Norden's Map, 1607

The exact date of the erection of the previous New Lodge is not recorded, although it was mentioned by a surveyor in 1537. Sometime prior to this a residence called *Hounds Lodge* stood on the site and was reported to be the home of Lord Raleigh. This building was situated near to the Royal Kennels in the Forest and undoubtedly had hunting connections. The likelihood is that it was originally a hunting lodge for the early kings.

An area created from part of the deforested Bray Wood between 1608 and

1650 was the 100 acre New Lodge Plain which was used for cavalry exercises. There is a record of a cavalry officer in 1800 facing a court martial because he saved a child's life during a brigade charge. Under the Van de Weyers, this area between new Lodge and Oakley Green was termed the Braywood Estate and had entrance lodges at Oakley Green bearing the Van de Weyer crest. Several other buildings in the village also bear the crest and were homes for the estate workers. In 1866 Madame Van de Weyer built a cruciform church on the estate which has now been demolished. It comprised a chancel, a nave, north and south trancepts, a tower and a porch, and provided the focus for the ecclesiastical parish of All Saints, Braywood formed in 1871. The churchyard still survives with the family tombs, including that of Jean Sylvain Van de Weyer who died in 1874 aged 72.

In common with most medieval settlements, the name of Oakley appears in many different forms, due to widespread illiteracy amongst the early inhabitants. Examples are *Aukeley (1220), Acle (1296), Ocle (1305), Okle (1375), Ockley (1572),* and later *Okeley* and *Oakley.* These all occur in legal and official documents, where in each case the lawyer or clerk was uncertain of the correct spelling.

The original village of Oakley Green was located on the Saxon and later packhorse route linking Windsor with Reading, now represented by the B3024 modern road. The Green itself was an area of common land on either side of the road where villagers grazed their animals. Kimbers Farm, located in the village, was mentioned in the year 1288 when it belonged to Walter Wodeward of Oakley. An ancient homestead moat at Mills Farm represents the old house of *Sheeres*, which is reputed to have been an inn for packhorse travellers. The Old Malt House, at the eastern extremity of the hamlet, was originally the 15th century Nags Head Inn.

Van Weyer Graves

East Oakley, as the name suggests, is represented by the area east of Oakley Green which extends northwards to Bullocks Hatch Bridge and the Willows. The most interesting building in this area is Bishop's Farmhouse, built as a hall house in the

15th century. However, records of *Bishop's* date back to 1288 when Michael Bishop held the property. The family seems to have been resident for nearly 500 years, with Elizabeth Bishop still holding the property in 1707. The Bishops also seem to have been involved with the neighbouring estate of Bullocks Hatch held by Robert Bullock in 1292. There was a water mill at East Oakley in 1451, when it was recorded that Robert West took excessive toll.

Water Oakley is a long, narrow settlement extending from Bullocks Hatch Bridge in the east to Builders Cross in the west. These two points lay on the A308 road which marks the boundary to the south, whilst the Thames bounds the area to the north.

Water Oakley has never been a highly populated area and undoubtedly owes its existence to the wharf which once stood on the site of Oakley Court. Being close to Windsor Forest, it was probably extensively used for the despatch of timber over many centuries, and one document of 1535 records that 'the Bishop of Winchester shipped quantities of oak from his estate at Billingbear in Windsor Forest from Water Oakley'.

The Wharf, however, was in use at a much earlier period. The first reference appears to have been in 1305 when Robert Glodeman is listed as 'the collector of tolls at Ocle'. By 1333 Reginal Belen was the tithingman and toll collector, and in that year he 'paid the sum of eight shillings for sixteen boats which had passed in the course of a year'. In 1373 John Cur, a local businessman, 'gave to the lord of the manor four shillings per annum for wharfage at Okle'.

After Down Place was built the land on which Oakley Court now stands, together with the Wharf, became part of the estate of that mansion. Sir Robert Jones bought Down Place in 1518 and the conveyance records that 'in that year Richard Weston granted to Sir Robert Jones a piece of land called *Queenes-Warfe* lying between Down Place on the west and his land called *Bawdwyne Botelers* on the east'. This probably requires some explanation.

Queens Wharf is the earlier title for Water Oakley Wharf, and probably takes its name from the same source as Queens Eyot, a small island in the Thames close to the Court. The prefix Queens is likely to allude to the fact that Bray was a royal manor, and that

New Lodge

C.J.

Oakley Court

C.J.

for a long period the land was always vested in the Queen consort. The reference to the land called 'Bawdwyne Botelers' is yet another example of local illiteracy. The person in question, who owned the land in 1498, was the Bray Parish Clerk Baldwin Boteler. His name, in turn, probably originated from the time when names and trades were often linked, ie Baldwin the bottler, though what his family bottled is not known.

In 1627 John Page of Down Place owned Oakley Wharf, of which James Ewst is listed as tenant, and for some time after that it was referred to as 'Page's timber wharf'. By 1800 maps show that a small community had built up around the landing place, and whilst one might be tempted to call this a village, it was probably made up of workers on the Down Place estate. However, Norden's map of 1607 clearly shows the existence of a village to the east of Oakley Court, with several houses and access to the main road. But today, apart from a small estate of houses near Bray Studios, the settlement of Water Oakley has dwindled and has now taken on the status of a postal district.

Oakley Court was originally erected for Richard Hall-Saye, J.P., in 1859 on land he purchased from the adjoining estate of Down Place. There is no record of the name of the architect, but he may be the same person who designed New Lodge, one mile to the south, which was completed in 1857. Mr Hall-Saye was born at Downham, Norfolk in 1827 and assumed the surname and arms of Saye in conformity with the will of his uncle, the Rev. Henry Saye, when he died in 1855. He travelled to Bray where he met and married Ellen Evans of Boveney Court, Bucks, in August 1857, a union from which came two sons and four daughters. He was appointed High Sheriff of Berkshire in 1864 and a Justice of the Peace in 1865.

Charles Kerry visited Oakley Court in 1861 and wrote: '*This Gothic mansion, the seat of Richard Hall-Saye, was erected on the ground formerly called Queens or Water Oakley Wharf, mentioned in the account of Down Place. The building is an admirable specimen of the adaption of the ancient baronial style to the requirements of the 19th century. The hall is spacious and contains a staircase of medieval design. The furniture throughout is oak. In a window in the library are the arms of Saye and Morley in stained glass*'

Another writer described it as a '*Victorian Neo-Gothic building with stock brickwork, regular black pointed jointing and stone quoins. Timber windows have been fitted into stone mullions. The stone fascias and friezes are extensively decorated. Gargoyles with forked tails, scaled bodies and ferocious muzzle jaws can be seen on the apex and the sides of the spires which abound. The building has steep gable roofs with a castellated tower to one side*'.

Mr Hall-Saye sold the estate in Spring 1874 and moved to Ives Place, the old manor house which stood on the site of the present Maidenhead Town Hall. During the 'Great Fire of Maidenhead', which occurred the following year at Langton's Brewery, he proved himself a hero by saving all the horses in the brewery stables, and organising the removal of several hundred barrels of beer, which were stacked in the market place much to the delight of the local inhabitants.

The new owner of the Court was Lord Otto Fitzgerald, a peer of whom little seems to have been recorded. When he moved into the building in 1874 he decided to instal a telephone, and as a consequence telegraph wires were stretched across the river on to the Bucks bank. These were found to be low enough to annoy the passing bargemen and after many complaints the court ordered that they be raised to a height of 30 feet.

In November 1875 Lord Otto received permission to erect a waterwheel on the riverbank. This was in position for at least 20 years but seems to have disappeared without record. When he died in 1883 the estate passed to his widow, Lady Fitzgerald, who had sold it by 1895 to John Lewis Phipps. His was a short reign as by 1900 it was in the possession of Sir William Beilby Avery, of Avery Scales fame. Sir William had apparently bought the house to be near the royalty at Windsor, and held many garden parties in the hope of attracting them. Whether he was successful is not known, but many ladies and gentlemen of quality attended the parties, for which Sir William always engaged the Brigade of Guards band from Windsor barracks.

Sir William died in 1908 and Lady Avery continued living at the Court until 1916 when she sold it to Ernest Olivier of the Olivier Shipping Company, who paid £27,000 for the building plus 50 acres of woodland. During his lifetime he spent a further £20,000 on improvements to the Court. Mr Olivier was born of French parents in Izmir, Turkey

Yew Tree Cottage.

C.J.

91

Old Malt House

C.J.

and was described as a businessman, diplomat and public benefactor. For six months of the year he lived in Monte Carlo, where he acted in an honorary capacity as Turkish Consul. He frequently entertained ambassadors and diplomats at the Court, and as a courteous gesture flew the flag of the nation they represented. During the Second World War General de Gaulle was a frequent visitor, and it may be for this reason that it has been said that Oakley Court was used as the English Headquarters of the French Resistance.

Ernest Olivier lived at the Court until his death in 1965 when he was 100 years old. For the next 14 years the building was deserted and allowed to crumble and fall into disrepair by its absentee owners. At a later date a secret vault was discovered on the ground floor of the building and found to contain papers and documents relating to the Olivier family and dating from the years 1910 to 1935.

In 1950 Hammer Films took over Down Place, next door to Oakley Court, and turned it into Bray Studios. The close proximity of the Court to the studios, plus the fact that it took on a sinister Gothic appearance, eventually led to it being used as a location for a number of films including Half a Sixpence with Tommy Steele, Murder by Death with Peter Sellers, and the lighthearted St Trinians series, where the Court was home for a hundred delinquent schoolgirls.

In 1957 Hammer Films found its true vocation when it started to make modern versions of the classic horror stories, including those featuring Dracula, Frankenstein and the Wolf Man mainly starring Christopher Lee and Peter Cushing. Oakley Court became 'Dracula's Castle', and was seen by millions as the home of the world's most famous vampire. To obtain an eerie effect the directors used only candles to light the entire Court.

In 1979 the crumbling mansion was put on the market by the trustees of the Olivier family, and was purchased by the present owners who converted it into the hotel as we see it today.

Down Place, now better known as Bray Studios, is situated on the river bank next door to Oakley Court. The architecture of the house dates to c.1750, which was undoubtedly a period of major alterations. The origins, however, may lie in the 15th century as in 1518 the house passed to Sir Robert Jones. After his death in 1532 he left the property to his heir, David Morgan, and his widow Katherine.

By 1600 it was in the hands of the Page family who owned considerable tracts of land in the area including that on which Oakley Court now stands. Arthur Page died in 1610 leaving it to his brother Randolph. By 1627 John Page was the owner and in that year he leased it to Richard and Henry Powney.

In 1720 the mansion was bought by Jacob Tonson, a publisher and bookseller of some fame. At Down Place he held regular meetings of the Kit-Kat Club, which purported to be a gathering of 'men of wit and pleasure about town'. The members included the Earl of Dorset, the Duke of Marlborough and Lord Halifax, together with many other noblemen and gentlemen. Writers of the day, like Addison and Steele, frequented the meetings, and even the poets Alexander Pope and Dryden were involved.

But beneath the facade of literary joviality the Club had more sinister objectives, concerned with the defence of the House of Hanover. The political movement undoubtedly had its origins in the Glorious Revolution of 1688, but the Club itself was founded in 1700 by Jacob Tonson, who was the first elected secretary. The initial meetings took place at the 'Cat & Fiddle', Shire Lane, London, where the Landlord, one Christopher Cat, who gave his name to the Club, served the members with mutton pies.

At that time the Whigs foresaw that after the death of William III there might be a serious danger of a Jacobite movement, calculated to imperil the Protestant succession. The Club met more frequently and after William's death in 1703 Tonson bought a house at Barn Elms and built a special room for the meetings. When he moved to Down Place thirteen years later he built a similar room, which was still in use after his death in 1736. During the early days of the Club, Sir Godfrey Kneller had painted portraits of 43 of the members, and these were hung in Down Place until 1772, when Richard, the last of the Tonson dynasty, and M.P. for Windsor, died. At least 20 of the Kneller paintings can be seen in the National Portrait Gallery in London and others are at Beningborough Hall in Yorkshire. Sir Godfrey Kneller developed his own size of portrait measuring 36" X 28" and these are still known as the 'Kit-Kat' format.

Bishops Farmhouse

Down Place

C.J.

After the Tonsons the house passed to the Duke of Argyle, and then to Baker Church and John Huddlestone, all in the space of 30 years. In 1807 Henry Harford bought the estate and his family held it until 1935 when it was purchased by George Davis.

Hammer Films moved into the old mansion in 1950 and converted it into Bray Studios. A series of stages and outbuildings were added and film sets erected on the spot. The first film made at Bray was 'Cloudburst' and this was followed by a series of modest thrillers during the years 1951–6, which culminated in the very successful Quatermass films bringing new dimensions in horror.

Realising the market potential, Hammer changed their policy in 1957 and embarked on remakes of the classic horror films, bringing a sense of realism to the old stories. Tomato Ketchup ran freely at Down Place when they made the Dracula and Frankenstein series, and featured other old favourites like The Mummy and The Wolf Man. By 1968, when they had finished filming, there were not too many horrific stories left unfilmed.

Down Place is still part of Bray Studios, which nowadays provides various services to the Film and TV industries. In its lifetime the old house has entertained both gentry and film stars, with personalities as diverse as the Duke of Marlborough, Christopher Lee and Errol Flynn.

Monkey Island and its hotel is situated in the Thames some half a mile downstream from Bray Lock and not far as the river flows from Down Place. It is popularly assumed that the Island takes its name from the famous monkey paintings which can be seen in one of the hotel buildings, but it is more likely to have derived from the earlier title of 'Monks – Eyot', which suggests that is was originally land being used by monks, perhaps close to their fishery in the Thames. The nearest monks were close by on the Bucks bank near Bray Lock where the moated site of Amerden Bank was a cell of Merton Priory from 1197 to the Dissolution, holding from the outset '92 acres of land and an assart with fishing in the Thames'. Domesday evidence suggests that before the Norman Conquest Amerden was held by Stigand, the Archbishop of Canterbury.

From the late twelfth century the island was part of the Whiteknights estate, now the site of Reading University, who probably leased it to the monks. A similar situation existed in 1361, when the Bray Court Rolls record that the island is called 'Bournhames – Eyte', on a document entitling John Casse and John Tylehurst to use it for pasturage at a charge of two shillings and sixpence per annum. The name occurs again in a Public Record Office plan of 1640 when it is referred to as 'Burnham-Ayt'. Presumably before the Dissolution the island was in the hands of the manor of Burnham, or even Burnham Abbey which was inhabited by canonesses rather than monks.

The Island passed to the Englefield family in 1606, and at this time it would still have been possible to see the signs of medieval cultivation, including a series of fishponds, used for the storage of fish for consumption. Traces of these, however, were wiped out in 1666 after the Great Fire of London. Large quantities of Berkshire stone were shipped down river to the capital for the rebuilding of the city, and on the return journey the barges carried unwanted rubble and are known to have dumped it on islands in the Thames, including Monkey Island. This proved to be a blessing in disguise as it provided a solid foundation for building.

In 1738 Sir Francis Englefield sold the island to Charles Spencer, the third Duke of Marlborough. The Duke was a member of the sinister Kit-Kat Club which had been meeting at nearby Down Place since 1720, and it was while he was attending meetings that he first saw the potential of Monkey Island. At this time the land measured 1000 X 500 yards, and the Duke, being a keen sportsman, decided to build a lodge and a temple, both buildings associated with fishing.

The Duke inherited Blenheim Palace in 1744, and it was about this time that he engaged Palladian architect Robert Morris to design and erect the buildings at a cost of £8,756. The ninth Earl of Pembroke was also involved in the design of the Temple or Banquetting House and was paid £2,277 for his work during the years 1745–8. Working with Morris was George Mercer, an experienced mason, and the carver William Perritt. It was Perritt who was responsible for the stucco ceiling on the first floor of the Banquetting House, with mouldings and panels depicting marine subjects including Neptune, various mermaids and water sports.

The most notable craftsman employed was the artist Andieu de Clermont, who was responsible for the monkey paintings. Previously he had worked at Norford

Amerden Priory

C.J.

Monkey Island

100

Hall in Norfolk where he first used the idea of *Singeries*, which were painted scenes featuring monkeys instead of people. He used the same technique on the ceiling of the fishing lodge where he produced panels of monkeys shooting, punting and fishing. One scene parodies Raphael's Triumph of Galatea, and other panels feature classic legends like Narcissus and Leda and the Swan.

Lady Hertford visited Monkey Island soon after the completion of the buildings and was suitably unimpressed when she wrote:

> *'He has a small house upon it, whose outside represents a farm, the inside what you please; for the parlour, which is the only room in it except a kitchen, is painted upon the ceiling in grotesque, with monkeys fishing, shooting etc., and its sides are hung with paper. When a person sits in this room he cannot see the water, though the island is not above a stone's cast over; nor is he prevented from this by shade; for, except for six or eight walnut trees and a few orange trees in tubs, there is not a leaf upon the island; it arises entirely from the river running very much below its banks. There is another building which I think is called a temple …'*

By the early nineteenth century the two main structures were surrounded by an array of outbuildings, and these were still there when the island was turned into an hotel in 1840. By the time Mrs Plummer was running the hotel in 1908 it had become a fashionable spot, especially after Edward VII and Queen Alexandra had regularly taken tea on the lawns accompanied by the next three reigning monarchs.

One of the Monkey Paintings

Other visitors at this time included Edward Elgar who composed his violin concerto in 1910 in the house called The Hut on the riverbank facing the hotel. This house was later renamed the Long White Cloud and was the home of the racing driver Sterling Moss. Musical stars Clara Butt and Nellie Melba were also entertained here. Rebecca West and her lover, H G Wells, were frequent visitors to the island after 1912, and Miss West's first novel 'Return of the Soldier' was set on Monkey Island, the heroine being the daughter of the innkeeper.

One story of the island concerns a monkey called Jacko who was chained to a walnut tree in an attempt to promote the hotel. He apparently escaped and so terrified a pregnant woman in Bray that her son was stillborn. Another anecdote is of the Irish ferryman who conveyed visitors to the Island before the bridge was built in 1956. He expected a glass of Guinness every twenty minutes, and if the drinks were not forthcoming he would take the boat back to the shore and leave the visitors behind.

Major alterations took place in 1963 when the dining area of the hotel was increased by the addition of a large glass-sided building which included a tree and a fishpool. In 1970 the Marlborough Room was added at the upstream end which had walls decorated with battle scenes. In the same year the Temple was extended to provide 30 extra bedrooms. In 1986 the then owner, Major Fitzwilliams, sold the island to Mr Basil Faidi, who consulted English Heritage over the restoration of the buildings.

Adjacent to Oakley Green is Fifield, a mainly linear settlement linking Builders Cross with the B3024. The village is of some antiquity being mentioned in 1316 as *Fifhide*. This is a fairly common name translating as 'five hides' which represents 600 acres of land. The oldest part of the settlement is probably Coningsby Lane where properties date back to the 15th century. These include Old Lodge Farmhouse and Yew Tree Cottage. The latter was originally a hall house and possibly an ancient manor. The yew tree to which the name refers had to be cut down recently after severe gales. In 1442 a hospital with almshouses was founded in the village.

CHAPTER VIII

Holyport and South Bray

Mention has been made of the importance of Holyport in medieval times as a market centre. Today this small hamlet shows no sign of this early activity which probably centred around the village green. In modern times the settlement has expanded to the north with modern housing and a small industrial estate alongside the M4 motorway which has sliced the Hundred of Bray into two halves.

During the medieval period it was under the control of the St Philibert family whose manor house was situated in a compound at the north end of Holyport Street. The only relics of its former existence are the dried-up moat which once surrounded the building and a free-standing tower. The last house on the site, which was named *Philberds* was demolished early this century, and succeeded two previous buildings. During its existence it housed the Goddards, the Wilcox's and the Beckinghams.

The second building was standing during the reign of Charles II (1649–85), and at one time was the home of

Philberds Tower

Nell Gwyn, his mistress. The King had first seen Nell on the stage and had invited her to supper. In 1670 she gave birth to his son, and in the presence of the King called him a bastard, pleading that she had no other name to call him. Charles took the hint and created him Earl of Burford and later Duke of St Albans. Nell was installed in Burford House, close by the walls of Windsor Castle and later at Philberds mansion. Whilst in Windsor the King often dined in the Duke's Head in Peascod Street with his wayward friend, George Villiers, Duke of Buckingham, who lived at Cliveden. Together they would ride to Holyport to visit Nell. She died in November 1687 and was buried in St Martins-in-the-field. For many years a bust of the lady stood in Philberds House but was eventually transferred to Bramshill House, Hants. A bell which belonged to her was sold at a local auction.

At one time there was a pair of stocks and a whipping post in Philberts Pound, and another set on the village green. Holyport Street, which led to the old mansion, was probably the main street in the medieval period, and is flanked by many early listed buildings. These include the 14th century Hamble Cottage, originally a hall house. Anne Duel's house and Coventry Cottage date to a century later and Goffs Cottage and Ivy Cottage are late 16th century. The 'Belgian Arms' public house was originally called 'The Eagle' but had its name changed because prisoners-of-war saluted the building as they passed by.

The village green today measures about eleven acres and at one time was common pasture. This right seems to have ceased at the time of Enclosure in 1817. Throughout history it has been used for many celebrations, including the fiftieth year of the reign of George III when free beer was distributed. Bonfires and fireworks were lit as a demonstration of local sympathy to the Queen of George IV on her acquittal. An unusual occurrence happened on 4th May, 1804, when a cloudburst deluged the Green and local resident Timothy Hughes was drowned.

On the south side of the Green there is a group of interesting buildings. The George Inn, which was originally a cottage, was built in the late 16th century.

The Brewhouse

The George

Hamble Cottage

The Brewhouse, which stands next to the inn, is now a general storehouse and is late 18th century. To the east of these is the attractive house called The Rails which was built in the mid-16th century. To the north of the Green is Holyport Lodge in whose grounds the Real Tennis Court was built in 1889 by Joseph Bickley (1835–1923), renowned for his patent method of constructing the wall and floor finishes for tennis and racket's courts. This is a rather unique building and still exists today as the Royal County of Berks Real Tennis Club. It was originally built for Samuel Heilbut in a utilitarian Queen Anne style. It is constructed of red brick and had a built-in swimming bath. The whole court is enclosed and measures 110 feet by 38 feet with 7 high windows on each side. The first game played in 1890 was between Samuel Heilbut and William Yardley, and the resident professional was John McCann. In the early days nearly all great amateurs and professionals played tennis on this court.

Ruins of the Wesleyan Chapel

Leaving Holyport by the Ascot Road the ruins of the Wesleyan Chapel built in 1835 can be seen on the west side. The bridge over the Bourne stream on the edge of the village was termed *Holyporte Brygge* in 1503. Almost immediately to the right is the small settlement of Stud Green, whose origins have always been a bit of a mystery. On the face of it this small settlement of houses appears as an unexplained cul-de-sac, but there may be some clues in the name. The prefix *Stud* can be traced back to 1761 and may have some connection with horses, but the original name was *Stert Green*, and it is listed as such in surveys of the common lands in Bray. A survey of 1608 shows it as 40 acres in size and another in 1650 as 20 acres. On a map appended to a further survey of

Royal County of Berks Real Tennis Club

107

Foxleys Manor dated 1624, it is shown as a large area of common land with no buildings.

The possibility is that in the 17th century *Stert Green* was common grazing and was completely devoid of houses or buildings of any kind. The earliest record of the name is in 1297, but in 1333 the names *Willus atte Sterte* and *Willus atte Strete* appear in the same year. Both the words *Strete* and *Stert* signify a street and indicate that the common must have had a right of way across it. A logical progression of the modern Stud Green is a bridle path leading to Ockwells and Lowbrooks manor houses at Cox Green and could conceivably have been a short cut between these manors, the manor of Foxleys, and Windsor.

The houses that we see at Stud Green today, with one exception, do not predate 1700, indicating that there was no settlement before that date. The exception is Stud Green Farmhouse which can be dated to c.1600, and may well have stood on its own at the west end of the Green. During the 19th century a brick industry developed in this small hamlet and provided work for many of the inhabitants. To the north of the road are a series of lakes which represent the area where clay was excavated for brick manufacture. One of the houses there was originally the 'Brickmakers Arms' public house, where the locals could buy a pint of ale to help lay the brick-dust.

Brickmakers Arms

Touchen End is the next hamlet along the road leading to Ascot, which lies on the old Saxon road and the border of Bray and Waltham parishes. The name is a shortening of *Tutchin Lane End c.1711* and signifies the place where Tutchin Lane, part of the Ascot Road, finishes. The ancient name of the settlement in 1274 was *Twychene*, meaning 'two chains', and this alludes to the chains placed across the fork of the roads leading to Hawthorne Hill and White Waltham, possibly as some sort of turnpike. In 1360 this area was listed as a tithing when the name *Iwhurst* is substituted. There was a family of that name living there for nearly 300 years, commencing with John de Iwhurst in 1293 and continuing until 1540.

Rails

C.J.

Stud Green Farmhouse

In 1607 Twychene is part of *Fines Bailiwick*, a large area of Windsor Forest, owned by the manor of Feens and Woolley situated on the edge of Maidenhead Thicket. An ancient route from Touchen End to Woolley can be traced via Paley Street, Heywoods Manor and Breadcroft Lane.

Touchen End is now a hamlet, but once had the church of Holy Trinity which was built about 1860, as a school licensed for public worship. This building has now been turned into houses. George III is said to have witnessed the death of a stag for the first time at Touchen End, where the ancient ceremony of spotting the Prince's face with the blood was performed by the chief huntsman. The deer was caught and killed in Price's Pond, which lay in the open green in front of the 'Hinds Head'. This may have been how the inn got its name.

Touchen End was termed in medieval times to be situated at 'Braywoodside', the other side of which was Moneyrow Green, a natural extension of Holyport. The origins of this settlement are ancient if obscure, the earliest mention being in 1376 when it was termed *Moneyrewe*. The size of the Green was 30 acres in 1608. On the south side of the Green, and opposite the end of Blackbird Lane stood a large and ancient house called *Sheers*. By tradition this was an inn on the packhorse route between Windsor and Reading.

Tradition has also fixed the story of King James and the Tinker at an inn called 'The Royal Blackbirds' in Blackbird Lane. Apparently the King, whilst hunting fallow deer, rode off on his own and stopped at an alehouse. Here he met a tinker who did not recognise him and they drank and joked together for many hours. Eventually the tinker, whose name was John of the Vale, said he would like to meet the King. The King, amused by this, offered to introduce him and rode with him to New Lodge. When the tinker realised that he was already in the presence of the monarch he begged for mercy. King James, who had enjoyed the charade, knighted the tinker as Sir John.

Moneyrow Green Post Box

Hawthorn Hill lies at the most southerly point of Bray Hundred on the border with White Waltham. This was the border that was under dispute for such a long period. It was marked with a Red Stone from which Redstone Farm, on the Drift Road, took its name. The farm was one of several in the area which belonged the Headington family, who in turn took their name from the manor of Headington, near Oxford, from where stone was quarried to build the walls of Windsor Castle in the 13th century.

The lands of Hawthorn Hill were mainly comprised of those belonging to Redstone Farm. It was Mr Headington who converted the farm into a racecourse, and the farm buildings into the HQ of the racing company. Originally the course was designed for the Royal Buckhounds and many a time the Prince of Wales, later Edward VII attended. It was converted for horses in 1887 and was at first used for military riders. Two three-day meetings were held each year in the Spring and November, and proved very popular. The April Household Brigade meeting, open only to amateur riders, also proved a great attraction. These meetings ceased in 1939, but after the war pony racing was held at the track for many years.

Hawthorn Hill is not thought to be named after the tree of the same name. Variations of the name are *Horethorn* in 1327 and *Hoe-thorne* in 1607 and may relate to a boundary mark. There was a Hawthorne family who may have taken their name from the settlement and William Hawthorne was listed as a church warden in 1600.

There was a wayside inn at Hawthorn Hill called 'The Woodman' of which the following legend is told:

"Many years ago, a certain inhabitant of Hawthorn was admonished in a dream to repair to London Bridge, where he was informed he should hear of something to his advantage. As the vision was thrice repeated, the warning was not disregarded. Having waited on the bridge a considerable time, he was at length accosted by a citizen, who, having heard the nature of his mission, advised him to return, and take no further notice of the affair; for he also had been recommended in a dream to go to a certain place called Hawthorn, where, beneath a venerable thorn was deposited a pot of gold, but where that place was he could not ascertain. Our traveller made no reply, but speedily returned to Hawthorn, where in the place intimated by the citizen, he discovered the hidden treasure. Some time afterwards, two scholars from Oxford, happening to call at his house for refreshment, observed the pot on the shelf, and carefully examined it. The vessel was surrounded by a Latin inscription, which for the benefit of their

unlettered host, they thus translated:

'Beneath the place where this pot stood,
There is another, twice as good.'

According to tradition, a second search proved both the truth of the inscription
and the accuracy of the translation. The worthy innkeeper suddenly grew rich
and prosperous, and the house, which for years had borne the sign of The
Woodman was ever afterwards called The Money Pot."

Before leaving the Holyport area brief mention should be made of the airfield which
was situated by the junction of the Holyport and Windsor Roads on land belonging to
the Good family of Stroud Farm. It was known as Maidenhead Aerodrome and was
opened 8th June, 1929. The entrepreneur behind this venture was Donald Stevenson,
who had a business at Station Approach, Maidenhead. However, the airfield was to
prove a four month wonder and was closed in October of the same year.

C.J.

Nell Gwyn

114

CHAPTER IX
Cox Green & Boyn Hill

The area as yet not discussed is the western section of the old Bray Hundred which has now been incorporated into the Borough of Maidenhead. Several small communities including Cox Green, Altwood, Tittle Row and Boyn Hill are now linked together by housing, but at one time were separate settlements under the control of the manor and parish of Bray. The area includes two large houses, on sites of former manor houses, which merit special mention.

The house that retains the name of Shoppenhangers Manor has an old world appearance but was actually built in 1915 to represent a 16th century merchant's house. It was the brainchild of Walter George Thornton-Smith, an antique dealer who moved to the area from Sussex. He was an expert at restoring houses and always insisted on authentic materials. To this end he brought in oak timbers by the dozen from ancient ships and the neighbouring Foxleys Manor. Materials for the interior came from West Wycombe and a unique and historic ceiling was imported from the Reindeer Inn at Banbury. Painted glass which had been rescued from a fire in 1790 at Selby Abbey arrived in boxes in which they had been stored for over 100 years.

The old barns were turned into workshops and many builders, carpenters and masons worked in them refurbishing genuine antiques for the interior of the house. Thornton-Smith presided throughout and when the building was completed and furnished it was as near authentic as it could be. A few years after completion the mansion at Billingbear Park was dismantled and an additional wing was added to

Shoppenhangers, with stone mullions, carvings, panelling and other materials obtained from this source.

Disaster struck in 1931 when a fire broke out on the first floor of the house, causing considerable damage there and in the roof. The magnificent moulded ceiling from Banbury collapsed in the drawing room, largely due to the weight of the water. £15,000 was spent on restoration which was mainly carried out by the original craftsmen. Thornton-Smith died in 1963 and from that date the house has been associated with the adjacent hotel.

Ockwells Manor House was originally built between 1446 and 1466 for Sir John Norreys. It still remains a very fine example of a house of this period with gatehouse, stables, barns and a dovecote. It was extended and altered in the 16th and 17th centuries and again in the 19th century by Fairfax Wade. It was restored again in 1986 by O Mansfield Thomas and Partners. The manor house stayed in the hands of the Norreys family until at least 1517 after which it passed to Sir Thomas Fettiplace. Bessils Fettiplace sold it to Thomas Ridley and others in 1583 but in 1587 it was purchased by William Day and his wife. By 1679 it was with the Finch family and was bought from them in 1786 by Penyston Portlock Powney. Eventually it passed with other manors to the Grenfell family.

Cox Green is one of those settlements whose name seems to defy interpretation, and may well have to remain that way. As a normal rule most local place names can be traced back to the Anglo-Saxon dialect and when translated provide an adequate and explainable description of the site. But who or what was Cox? That is the question that needs to be answered if the mystery is to be solved.

Evidence seems to indicate that the name did not come into use until the late 18th century, and early maps show it to be an area of arable land within the manor and parish of Bray. The main development period occurred after the second World War and since then thousands of houses have been erected and Cox Green has become an entity in its own right with a community centre in Highfield Lane. Not surprising perhaps as the A423 motorway spur, which began in 1939 as the Maidenhead Bypass, separated

Cox's Cottages

Old Thatch

the settlement from the rest of Maidenhead, placing Cox Green fairly and squarely south of the border.

The first mention of any properties in the area of Cox Green occurs in a grant of 1621 from a charity set up by Sir John Norreys of Ockwells Manor. Houses were to be provided for 'all poor, aged or impotent persons of Bray Parish to live in certain parcels of ground', and six of the cottages were located somewhere near to the Foresters public house. The first two were in the possession of Anne Clayton (1799) and William Clayton (1817), ancestors of the well known Cox Green family. Others belonged to Thomas Johnson (1799), Matthew Sawyer (1699) and Richard Franklyn (1699). The administrator of the charity was one Thomas Wilcox, whose name if shortened through illiteracy from Thomas William Cox, could conceivably have given his name to the settlement.

By map evidence Cox Green, together with its name, seems to have come into being between the years 1792 and 1817. An enclosure map of 1817 specifically names the settlement and shows 18 houses in existence situated on both sides of Cox Green Lane. In 1761 a few houses were sited between the Foresters and Lock Lane, while the area west of the Green was part of Maidenhead thicket.

Any development of Cox Green was prohibited until 1815 by the existence of Maidenhead

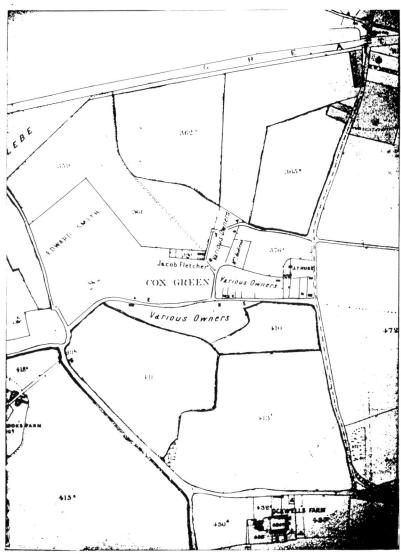

Grenfell Estate Map c.1877

Racecourse. This stretched from Tittle Row to Cox Green and was quite large in extent as races were run over two and four miles. The course was certainly there in 1754 as a racecard exists. In 1768 the King of Denmark attended the races and in 1767 Mrs Philip Powys records in her diary that George III and the whole royal family were present. There is also a record of their attending on 27th September, 1787. The 'Royal Calender', which was first published in 1773, contains the Maidenhead fixture for that and every subsequent year down to 1787. The fixture was usually a three day event taking place each September. There is a gap in the records from 1787 to 1801 when Mr Spencer's bay mare, Luisa, beat Mr Smith's chestnut filly Don Quixote. The races seemed to have ceased by 1815.

On the edge of the Thicket at the west end of Cox Green Lane stood the residence of Old Court which seems to have been of some antiquity. This large house, which was taken over by British Filters in April 1944, may have stood on the site of the Court of the Canons of Waltham Abbey, who held the manors of Heywoods at Woodlands Park. Cannon (Canon) Lane, which was linked to Old Court by Highfield Lane, was also an old route used by the Waltham Canons.

Having established that a small hamlet existed by about 1800, we can now give further consideration to the name. The Green, which is still extant although perhaps diminished in size, would be a piece of common land where animals could graze, perhaps when being driven to market. The prefix

MAIDENHEAD RACES.

TUESDAY, October 10, 1775.

The Ladies Purse of Fifty Pounds, (the best of Three Four-Mile Heats) by any Horse, Mare or Gelding ; Five Year Olds, to carry 8st 8lb. Six Year Olds, to carry 8st. 12lb. and Aged Horses to carry 9st. 3lb. Those that have won one 50l. Plate this Year to carry 3lb. extraordinary, those that have won two 50l. Plates this Year, to carry 5lb. extraordinary, and those that have won three or more 50l. Plates this Year, to carry 7lb. extraordinary.

	RIDER's Names and the Colours of their Dress.	1st Heat.	2d Heat.	3d Heat.
MR. Brown's br horse, Crony, aged, (3 plates) 9st. 10lb.	William Barnes, Blue.	2	2	
Mr. Rider's bay gelding, Casca, 6 years old, 8st. 12lb.	John Rider, Purple.	dif.		
Mr. Gwyn's ch. h. Culprit, 6 years old, (1 plate) 9st 1lb.	Rider unknown.	4	dr.	
Mr. Jennings's bay horse, Nestor, aged, (2 plates) 9st. 8lb.	Thomas Garret, Orange.	3	4	
Mr. Dymock's bay horse, Zachary, aged, 9st. 3lb	J Reynard, Blue & White.	6	dr.	
Mr. Stacey's Fortune Hunter, 5 yrs. old, (2 plates 8st. 12lb.	R. Lefenby, Bl & White.	1	1	
Capt. O'Kelly's b. h. Cassimus, 5 years old, (1 plate) 8st. 11lb.	Samuel Merrit, Red.	5	3	

WEDNESDAY, October 11.

The TOWN Purse of Fifty Pounds (the best of three Two Mile Heats) by any Horse, &c not exceeding Four Years old last Grass ; Colts to carry 8st. 4lb. and Fillies 8st. 0lb. and those that have won one 50l. Plate this Year to carry 3lb. extraordinary, those that have won two 50l. Plates this Year, to carry 7lb. extraordinary, and those that have won three or more 50l. Plates this Year, to carry 10lb. extraordinary.

	RIDER's Names	1st	2d	3d
LORD Castlehaven's grey colt, Bosphorus, 8st. 4lb.	Edmund Allen, Red.			
Mr. Adams's dun colt, Dunny : 2 plates 8st. 11lb.	William Bristow, Crimson.			
Mr. Green's bay colt, Trimmer, 8st. 4lb.	John South, Yellow.			
Mr. Duggins's bay colt, Lightfoot, (one plate) 8st. 8lb.	William Barnes, Striped.			
Mr. Tomb's bay colt Codrus, (one plate) 8st. 8lb.	Unknown.			
Mr. Stephenson's grey colt, (to be sold) 8st. 4lb.	Unknown.			
Mr. Rider's black colt, Ivory Black, 8st. 4lb.	John Talbot, Purple.			
Mr. Langbridge's grey colt, Burntcrust, 8st. 4lb.	John Brown, Yellow.			
Capt. Bertie's bay filley, Lady Catchet, 8st.	William Blois, Yellow.			
Capt. O'Kelly's chesnut filley, Juno, 8st.	Giles Edwards, Red.			

THURSDAY, October 12

The NOBLEMEN and GENTLEMENS Subscription Purse of Fifty Pounds, Give and take, free for any Horse, &c. Aged Horses to carry 8st. 4 Hands to carry 7lb. and to allow 7lb. for every Year under ; and to carry 3lb. extraordinary for every Plate they shall have won this Year.

	RIDER's Names	1st	2d
MR. Tilbury's grey mare, Melissa, 6 years old, (1 plate) 13 hands, 1 inches, 1 half, 1-8th.—8st. 0lb. 6z.	Thomas Campbell, White.	1	2
Mr. Watts's bay horse, Gudgeon, aged, 14h.—8st. 7lb.	William Grifton, Crimson.		

•.• To start at One o'Clock.

Maidenhead Races

Cox, bearing in mind the late development of the settlement, is most likely to be a personal name. A check through the Bray records shows that there are at least 25 entries of the name between the years 1662 and 1797. Sometimes the spelling is *Cocks* or *Cochs*, but it is not unusual for the letters ch to be replaced by an x, being the Greek symbol for the first two letters of Christ's name, as in the shortened word Xmas.

Some proof of Cox being a personal name comes from a row of old dwellings in Lock Lane known as Cox's Cottages, which appears to indicate that they were built by or for a person called Cox. An extensive search, however, has not revealed any landowner or noteworthy person of that name, unless it was the aforementioned Thomas Wilcox. One long shot is that there may be some connection with Richard Cox (1777–1845) who developed the Cox's Orange Pippin. This famous apple came from a strain of the Ribstone Pippin and was first recognised in 1825 at the Colnbrook nursery of a Mr Smale.

Could it be that William Cox conducted some early trials at Cox Green? There were certainly extensive market gardens and orchards there where a variety of apples were grown, many of which are immortalised in the road names of the Apple Estate built by Sunway Homes. A further coincidence is that the Smale family were developers in Cox Green and built some large properties in Highfield Lane.

The Brill family were farmers and fruit growers over a long period in Cox Green where they leased large areas of land and owned several houses, including Rose Cottages which were built for their workers. They also developed the Brilson herd of Wessex Saddleback pigs which lived in the orchard paddocks and in pigsties at Common Farm, now Stratford Gardens. Wessex Way is named after these pigs, although the other roads on the council estate are called after Saxon kingdoms, towns and saints. The Brills still live at Homer Farm in Cox Green Lane.

Next to Homer Farm is Beehive Manor, which was also associated with the Brill family. One of their number is said to have been the innkeeper when this building was the Dog and Partridge. At that time it was a two-storey building which was later converted into a farmhouse and bakery. The name comes from the beehives which were placed in the garden by a Mr Haynes, while the manor suffix was added as a status symbol.

In the early 20th century it was held by a Mrs Hyde, an antique dealer, who sold it to Mr Appleton, a millionaire, who extended the building and added a third storey. In the 1930s it was a weekend home with many showbiz parties being held there.

Victory Hall

Appleton went broke about 1940 and moved in with his butler and cook, Mr and Mrs Lightfoot, as their lodger! During the war the manor was let to the Duke of Manchester after a German family had been hounded out, and was then converted into six flats. Clock Cottage, on the opposite side of the road, was built in 1936 with old timbers from a house in Stoke Poges, and was briefly let to Jim Mollison, husband of Amy Mollison, the well known pilot.

The nucleus of Cox Green was situated close to the Green itself, and down Lock Lane, named after Grannie Lock who lived in a thatched cottage there. The Foresters and the Barley Mow were the two local pubs. The Post Office was built in 1939 at the time that the settlement was cut off from Maidenhead. Where Sherbourne Drive is now there was a house owned by Mrs Fletcher and a small holding in the possession of the Vanes who owned Ellay Tubes. During the Festival of Britain in 1951 the Vanes erected a skylon similar to that on the South Bank in London.

The Church of the Good Shepherd

Among those buildings that have disappeared from the landscape were Victory Hall and the Church of the Good Shepherd. The former was created after the first World War from an old army hut and was later used as a community centre for whist drives, film shows and dances. The earliest record of the church was in 1874 when it was a Primitive Methodist Chapel. It was purchased by All Saints in 1911 when an apse and porch were added, and became separated again from Boyn Hill in 1975. Both of these buildings were demolished

Clock Cottage

C.J.

Beehive Manor

124

and incorporated in the new community centre, built around 1970 from donations and the sale of the Victory Hall site.

One of the outlying residences was The Points, which was home to both Countess Annesley and Lady Fairfax. Another was Kimbers House, held by Mr and Mrs Ford, of blotting paper fame, in 1914. During the war the grounds were used to house German and Italian prisoners of war, and later for the Cox Green Flower Show which was organised annually for 37 years by the secretary, Mr Bedford. It was usually held on a Thursday and gardeners from 30 miles around came to exhibit their produce.

It was after the second World War that Cox Green expanded in all directions. To the east the Larchfield estate wiped out all but a fragment of Curls Lane. To the north the Wessex estate reached Highfield Lane, and to the south the Apple estate and Ockwells Park covered a majority of the open ground. The ancient Green was almost completely lost within the suburban sprawl.

Until the turn of the century Altwood was part of the Parish of Bray and was still in Royal hands in 1488 when it was part of the dowry of Queen Elizabeth, wife of Henry VII. However, it probably dates back to Domesday although the earliest record is in 1241 when it was spelt *Altewode*.

In a survey of 1650 it is described as an area of 220 acres of common woods belonging to the Manor of Bray, from which tenants had the right to take three loads of wood annually for use in the household. At this time the Beadle, or Court Usher, was allowed five loads of wood for executing his office.

In 1335 pannage fines were paid to the Court because someone allowed his pigs to feed for too long on the acorns and beech mast. These could conceivably have been some of the swine from Norden Farm. But not only the poor were punished, as in 1359 we find the Thomas de Foxley, the Constable of Windsor Castle, had to account for wrongly cutting down three beech trees in Altwood. All sections of Windsor Forest had a woodward, who was appointed to administer the woodland. In 1340 Roger de Colingborne looked after Altwood and in 1488 Andrew Wynch had the job. Later in 1504 Robert Norreys, of Ockwells Manor, held the position.

It is likely that Altwood was not as dense as one might at first suppose, but probably not unlike the Maidenhead Thicket of today. The name Altwood Bailey suggests that there was some sort of enclosure at this point and excavations in several house gardens in this road have revealed first and second century remains of corn drying kilns, a well and other features of the Roman period. These are thought to be outbuildings associated with the Cox Green Roman Villa nearby and are likely to have been situated in a forest clearing. We know too that there was at least one mansion in Altwood which had 47 acres of land attached to it. The estate was known as *Masts* and was purchased by Robert Little in 1530 from John March. He passed the estate on to his son Thomas.

Thomas Little was of some importance in the area, and employed workers on his estate. I like to think that he built the workers a row of houses which was called Thomas Little's Row, which later became shortened to Tittle Row. This may be wishful thinking however, as this small settlement at one end of Altwood Road is also recorded in the Bray Award of 1817 as both *Tittle-bag Row* and *Tickle-back Row*, both names which have a modernish ring about them. Although Tittle Row as a name does not specifically indicate antiquity the survey of 1650 lists 10 people who paid rent in this area which may then have been embraced by the name Altwood.

Old Smithy

There are, however, some ancient buildings there, the oldest of which is probably the Old Thatch, a 17th century timber framed structure with thatched roof which was at one time an inn or an ale house. This listed building is very impressive and may well be older than examination indicates. Close by is The Old Smithy, a dwelling house which was once a forge dating back to the 16th century with deeds which go back to 1625. At the rear of the buildings was the wheelwrights shop, while Berry Cottage, the house next door, was built in 1818 as a house for the Smith. From 1863 to 1883 the Smithy was run by Peter Silver, with the assistance of young Richard Silver, who went on to be an Alderman and Mayor of

Kimbers House

C. J.

Norden Farm

Maidenhead in 1872 and 1877. The forge was closed in 1920 when a Mr Butts converted it into a small residence.

At the east end of Altwood Road is Norden Farm. The name Norden in Old English means 'north woodland pasture' often associated with the pasturing of swine. This meaning applies even if Norden is a personal name, although the only locally recorded Norden I can find was the cartographer who carried out a survey of Windsor Castle and Forest in 1607. Nowadays the farm buildings are sandwiched between the Wootton Way Estate and the schools of Altwood and St Edmund Campion, which were all built on the original farm land. Two hundred years ago, however, the complex stood very much on its own to the north of the Altwood, once a section of the Windsor Forest. A map of 1761 shows that Maidenhead Thicket extended as far down as Boyn Valley Road.

It has to be said that we cannot be sure at what date it evolved. Wooden barns are notoriously difficult to date because they are patched up over the centuries. It may indeed have originated before the 18th century and perhaps a clue comes from the fact that Robert Challoner, who died in 1621, left a farm in Altwood in his will to Robert Fincher. Or perhaps we can tie in the 13th to 14th century pottery that was found in the farm precincts at the time of building the adjacent housing estate. Either way, the farm buildings as we see them today are a fine example of post medieval architecture.

On the opposite side of the road from Norden Farm is the house known as The Boynings, in which it is said that Isambard Kingdom Brunel lived temporarily whilst building the Great Western Railway between 1837 and 1840.

Before All Saints Church was built in 1857 the area known as Boyn Hill was completely devoid of buildings with the exception of Boyn Hill Farm, which was an ancient parcel of the Manor of Ives, in the tenure of the monks of Bisham. The Bray Court Rolls record that in 1520 'John Grove held

Boynings

129

the farm of the Prior and Convent of Bustleham (Bisham) in Maydenhith'. The name Boyn Hill referred to the whole area covered today by Boyndon, Westmorland, Clare, Boyn Valley and Laburnham Roads, as well as Boyn Hill Avenue and Kingsgrove. The latter was an area of Boyn Hill Farm and was listed in 1292 as *Kynngesgrove*, being land belonging to the King.

The earliest mention of the name *Boyn Hill* occurs in a survey of the Manor of Ives in 1550. Prior to this and in 1496 it as termed *Boyndon juxta (near) Altewode.* Use of the name *Boyndon*, which means the same as Boyn Hill, can be traced back to 1333 when Henry de Boyndon is listed as a tithingman. The prefix *Boyn* cannot be accurately explained, but similar names in Ireland are said to allude to a sacred white cow.

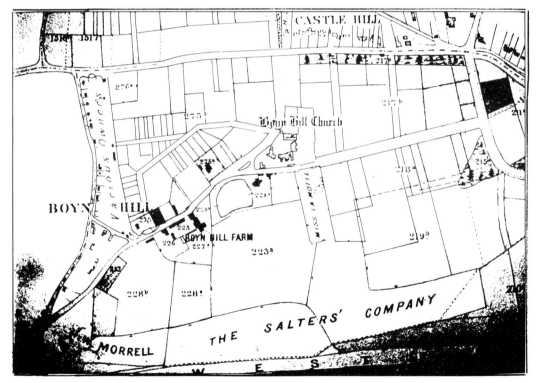

Grenfell Estate Map c.1877

Boyn Hill began to become populated after the building of All Saints Church. The choice of site for what was to be the first of the Victorian Anglican churches in Maidenhead, was chosen in 1854 by two spinsters Maria and Emily Hulme from Shinfield whose plan it was to found a church complex with a school and almshouses in a neighbourhood where they could reside and be associated with the running of the church.

The site for the complex was generously donated by Charles Pascoe Grenfell who owned virtually all the land in the area. The architect chosen was George Edmund Street (1824–81), listed among the top five mid-19th century English architects, who, amongst other things, was responsible for the design of London's Royal Courts of Justice. Street was well known to Bishop Wilberforce of Oxford, and had been appointed Diocesan architect in 1850.

Street's original design was for a double-aisled church with a spacious vicarage, coach house, stables, schoolrooms and a master's house, forming a group around three sides of a quadrangle. In addition he had designed a house nearby for the Hulme sisters. The foundation stone was laid on October 23rd, 1855 and the complete church consecrated by the Bishop of Oxford on December 2nd, 1857. The public response was so great that tickets had to be issued for those attending the ceremony. In the afternoon 150 invited guests were present at a luncheon where the vicar of Bray, the Rev. Austen-Leigh spoke of his pleasure in seeing the church erected at the western end of his parish.

The famous tower and spire, which are a landmark for many miles around, were not erected until 1864 due to lack of funds. The other major extension was in 1911 when the nave was extended westwards and a new porch erected. These alterations transformed the church into the edifice that we see today with seating for 550 people.

Exterior of All Saints' Church, Boyn-Hill, Maidenhead. c.1857

Life at All Saints was not without its dramatic moments. In 1858 the senior curate, Richard Temple West was accused of forcing confession from an ignorant woman, which created quite a scandal. A second incident took place ten years later, after the tower had been fitted with a peal of eight bells. A careless workman smoking his pipe inside the tower set fire to the woodwork causing a blaze fierce enough to melt the bells! Of famous people who visited the church one should perhaps mention Garibaldi, the Italian patriot, and Mr W H Gladstone, the Victorian politician.

Before leaving Boyn Hill mention should be made of the milestone on the south of the Bath Road and the end of All Saints graveyard. This is clearly marked with the words 'Bray Parish' and marks the northern extremity of old Bray Hundred. It is one of the surviving relics of this coaching era when horse-drawn vehicles rumbled by on their way from London to Bristol and Gloucester. The stone records Bath as 81 miles and Hyde Park Corner as 27.

Interior of All Saints' Church, Boyn-Hill, Maidenhead. c.1857

CHAPTER X

The Thames and Fisheries

The final and as yet undiscussed section of the Hundred of Bray is that area of the flood plain lying between Maidenhead Bridge and Bray Church, now mainly taken up with the Fisheries Estate. The history of this area is irrevocably linked with Bray waterfront and the river Thames, which before 1840 provided an important means of communication, as well as a source of food.

Mention has been made of the lack of mills and fisheries in the manor of Bray at Domesday. These resources, however, are to be found later and we find that in 1206 Jordan de London received from King John a grant of a farm and mill at Bray. In 1375 it is recorded that Robert Muleward of Bray Mill took excessive toll and in 1489 William Kember was guilty of the same offence. In 1770 it was called 'Levell's paper mill' and in 1794 Lavenders Mill, for grinding corn. Another mill at East Oakley was mentioned in 1451 when Robert West was also taking excessive toll.

The medieval fisheries in the Thames at Bray are listed as Maidenhead Bridge, Upper Garston Eyott, Amerden Ash, Down Place and Ruddle Pool. *Eyots, Aits or Ayts* were all names describing small islands and a Public Record Office plan dated 1640, and prepared in connection with one of the numerous fishery disputes, lists the following islands between Maidenhead Bridge and Ruddle Pool: *Garston Ayt, Headpile Ayt, Orchard ait, Felling ayt, Mill ayt, Coneygray ayt, Burnham ayt, Monkey Island, Cherry ayt, Spratwell ayt, Queens ayt, Cowley ayt, Warehouse ayt* and *Bullocks ayt*.

Another fishery, termed *Dedepole* in 1296, was situated inland on an old marsh called *Tadpool*. The large brook, known today as York Stream, flowed into this. In 1484 it took the name of *Dunmede Dyche* from a meadow of that name. Henry Staverton from Staverton Lodge was listed in 1485 as being one of the parties responsible for the cleansing of this brook. Another stream in the area was *Shaffel* or *Shortfordmoor* which originally discharged into the Thames at Garston's Mead under the name of *Hogge Bridge Stream*. This was later diverted when The Cut was formed in 1819.

Bray Lock seems to have been built in 1845. However, there was a lock there as early as 1377 called *Hameldon Lock*, where travellers once again complained about exorbitant toll. Both the lock and the weir were taken up in 1510, by order from the Commissioners of Sewers. A further lock, built by Thomas Manfield, was pulled up in 1622. There is another reference to a weir at this point in 1328 called *Braibrok*, occupied by Richard atte Lock of Bray on behalf of the Crown. All these early constructions are likely to have been flash locks. The earliest keeper at the present pound lock was James Fenemore, but the sides were not added to the lock until around 1870. In March 1883 the Thames Conservancy declined to reconstruct the tumbling bay to allow barges to pass through in flood time, but by 1885 they had rebuilt both the lock and the weir.

Prior to the building of the Great Western Railway in 1837 there were no buildings between Maidenhead Bridge and Bray Church. The iron road, like the M4 motorway, cut a swathe through the old Hundred of Bray and made general access more difficult.

Maidenhead's Riverside Station, which had opened in June 1838, was coping well with the increasing traffic, but Isambard Kingdom Brunel's priority was to continue the line to Bristol. To do this it was necessary to construct a bridge across the Thames, and work on this project began early in 1837 and was completed in October 1838 at a cost of £37,000.

Brunel's design for Maidenhead Railway Bridge was controversial and brought speculative comment from his rivals. When completed the total length of the bridge was 778 ft., with an original width of 30 ft. It comprised two wide arches, each 128 ft. in span, with a rise of 24 ft. 3 in.

Bray Lock   C.J.

Brunel Bridge

C.J.

At each end of the main span were four smaller arches which were to allow for floods and leave the towpath clear, the latter having been stipulated by the authorities. It was constructed by a Mr Chadwick, a contractor from London, who used stock bricks with cement and stone from quarries near Leeds.

The two side span arches, which had been included in the design to ensure that the navigational channel was not obstructed were, and still are, the largest spans of brickwork in the country. The central piers rested on a shoal in the centre of the river, now Guards Club Island. For several months after its completion many tons of stone were placed on the bridge to prevent any upward springing before it was completely set, and the centerings supporting the brickwork were left in position.

Brunel's critics were convinced that the wide brick arches would not stand and were delighted when in May 1838 the centerings were eased, and signs of distortion were seen in the eastern arch. Brunel inspected the bridge but the contractor admitted liability for the defect and rebuilt the distorted section.

Brunel ordered that the centerings be left in place for another winter, but during January 1840 the weather was bad and high winds blew the centerings down. There were also many violent storms and heavy rain which caused the Thames to rise by five inches. But despite these hazards the bridge stood firm and the critics were silenced for ever.

The Brunel Bridge was hailed as a masterpiece and a Victorian guidebook of 1862 quotes: 'To the eye familiar with geometric beauty the perfect execution of an elliptical arch, on so large a scale, and so high a degree of execution, is an uncommon gratification; but when the practical mechanician considers the difficulties and risks which must have attended its construction … then indeed, and only then, will he sufficiently appreciate the courage and the capacity which had approached so near the verge of possibility without transgressing its bounds.'

The painter, J.M.W. Turner, immortalised the bridge in 1844 when he painted 'Rain, Steam and Speed' which depicted a broad gauge train en route to Maidenhead.

The story goes that Turner was returning to London by train when he received the inspiration for his masterpiece. His travelling companion, one Lady Simon, described the event as follows:

> *'The old gentleman seemed strangely excited at this, jumping up to open the window, craning his neck out, and finally calling to her to come and observe a curious effect of light.*

> *A train was coming in our direction, through the blackness, over one of Brunel's bridges, and the effect of the locomotive, lit by crimson flame, and seen through driving rain and whirling tempest, gave a peculiar impression of power, speed and stress.'*

The bridge was widened in the 1880s to 60 ft. to provide more lines. The job was completed in January 1893 and opened again to traffic on 1st February 1893. The wide span arches were found to possess an echo, whereby words uttered on the towpath repeated eight times, and to this day the eastern arch is known locally as the Sounding Arch.

It was around 1880 that development commenced along the Bray riverside between the road and the rail bridges. The Thames Riviera Hotel was completed in 1886 as a castellated mansion house and converted into an hotel in 1888. Maidenhead Rowing Club, which stands adjacent to the hotel was founded in the 1870s and the present club buildings erected in 1897. It benefitted greatly from the interest shown by William Grenfell, a rower himself, who lived in Taplow Court which stands on the hill at the east end of the bridge.

Guards Club Road, which runs alongside the Waterside Lodge, leads to a riverside park of the same name which was landscaped by the Council and the Maidenhead Civic Society. This area was originally the site of the Brigade of Guards Club, and was the home of Guards officers from Windsor and Pirbright. The land was donated by Lord Cheylesmore in 1903 together with the residences of Edendale and Riverside, and an island in the centre of the river. Here the officers relaxed in comfort and rowed or

C.J.

Bray Lodge

Lillie Langtry

fished. Their regular Ascot Ball was always attended by the Queen and other members of the Royal Family.

Women were not allowed to stay at the Club and consequently many mistresses were installed in the houses now known as Gaiety Row on the Bucks bank directly opposite. When the Guards Club was demolished after 1965, the site was excavated by the Maidenhead Archaeological Society who found several discarded wedding rings amongst the rubbish! Today the Guards Club Park is for the public to enjoy and a metal bridge allows the visitor to cross onto the island where the officers took tea with their ladies in a summerhouse.

The land between the railway and Bray Church is that now occupied by the Fisheries estate which was built in 1890. Prior to the Enclosure in 1817 this land was known as *Oldfield* and was one of the common pastures of Bray Manor. In 1340 an inquest was held by the King to ascertain who had common rights throughout the year and was attended by Thomas de Foxle, John de Shobenhangre and Robert de Shyplake, all local names. In the days of Queen Elizabeth I archery meetings were held in the meadow and local men practiced there. One of these meetings is commemorated by a brass plate in Clewer Church which is inscribed:

> *'He that lieth under this stone,*
> *Shott with a hundred men alone,*
> *This is trew that I do say,*
> *The match was shott in Oulde Felde at Bray,*
> *I will tell you before you go hence*
> *That his name was Martine Expence.'*

In more modern times Old Field was used for cricket fixtures, and was the forerunner of the Maidenhead & Bray Cricket Club. At least two matches took place between Bray and the MCC. On one occasion when the Londoners heard the church bells sound their defeat they retired without partaking of the excellent meal provided for them.

In 1887 the Rev. Charles Raymond sold Old Field, recorded as 34 acres, to Mrs Annie Smith for £5,000. Mrs Smith already owned the osier beds on the river and had been

Annie Smiths Boundary Stone

living in her residence called 'The Fishery' since 1870. She was said to have been a wealthy eccentric who had a penchant for rare aquatic birds which she kept in an aviary on her land. She moved from the district after she had lost a rather expensive High Court Action over fishery rights in the Thames.

Before leaving Annie Smith sold the land for development in 1888. At this time the Fisheries Estate was developed, when a heron with a fish in its beak was used as a fisheries symbol. Polygonal pillars with terracotta herons, manufactured by local builder J K Cooper, were to be seen at all entrances to the estate.

A boundary stone marking the extent of Annie Smith's estate can be seen on the corner of Oldfield Road and Chauntry Road. This circular column has an embossed heron on it with Annie's initials on it in Old English and a series of Roman numerals making up the date 1890.

There are many large and attractive houses on the Fisheries Estate with lawns running down to the river. One such building is Bray Lodge, where it is reputed that Lillie Langtry, mistress of Edward VII, lived for a period. The Prince of Wales, or Bertie, as Lillie called him was classified as a rake. Apart from his women he liked good food and enormous cigars. He enjoyed mixing with society at Maidenhead, eating at Skindles and being entertained at parties at Taplow Court and Cliveden. He also attended Ascot Races on a regular basis.

Lillie Langtry, sometimes known as Jersey Lily, was born on the island of that name in 1853 and died in 1929.

Bray Church and the Fisheries 1791

Index to Selected People and Places